# My Breast Year Ever

## PAULA CANNY

Order this book online at www.trafford.com
or email orders@trafford.com

Most Trafford titles are also available at major online book retailers.

Note for Librarians: A cataloguing record for this book is available from Library
and Archives Canada at www.collectionscanada.ca/amicus/index-e.html

Cover Photo - Kevin Osmond
Editor - Woody Simmons

Printed in the United States of America.

ISBN: 978-1-4251-8644-9 (sc)

*Trafford rev. 12/01/2010*

 www.trafford.com

**North America & international**
toll-free: 1 888 232 4444 (USA & Canada)
phone: 250 383 6864 ♦ fax: 812 355 4082

For Woody, My Mother, and
For Anyone Who Has Had Cancer Of Any Kind, And
For Everyone Who Has Shared In the Experience.

# 1

# BEFORE I KNEW WHAT I HAD TO WORRY ABOUT

I worry. I worry that I am not good enough. I worry that I am not important. I worry that I am not respected. I worry that I worry. I do other things besides worry. But even when I do other things I worry about whatever it is that I am doing. Luckily I have had ADD for many years and developed an ability to do more than one thing at a time. As a child I did my homework watching TV. So I could do two things, actually three things at the same time, i.e. do homework, watch TV and worry. No one noticed that I worried when I watched TV and did my homework. They complained that I was doing two things at a time. No one considered that really I was doing even more than what they could see because I was worrying.

I worry that I do not have enough money. I worry that I will not make enough money. I worry about everyone making too much money, which is really just another way to describe that I worry that

I will not have enough. I have never worried that I will have too much of anything, except that I worry that I might get fat. I do not want to have too much me.

I worry that I may never meet Oprah Winfrey, among others, and how funny that I have for most of my life remained a size 6 to 8 and Oprah has not. I worry about Oprah and her challenges with her weight. I want her to not have the challenge and for her to be okay. I want for me to be okay and not worry about Oprah.

For a short time I was bigger than a size 6-8. That was the summer before my junior year in college. My father lost his job. My parents sold the family house in a suburb of Washington D.C. and we moved to Cape Cod. I ate luncheon meat every night at about 3 am after drinking lots of beer. And then I weighed about 130 pounds. I lost the weight within six months when I returned to college and then lost more weight when I went to London for a semester abroad. I got downright skinny just after turning 21 because I was raped four days before I turned 21. I stopped eating and only worried.

I had never really worried about being raped before I was raped. That is not what I worried about. Then I worried about everything without being able to identify anything. Now after years of therapy I concern myself less with generalities and worry more about particulars like whether Oprah will ever want to talk to me. I do not worry about whether I would want to talk to Oprah, though I would. That is a problem. I know it is and I worry about that.

I worry that I will never get to meet Vanessa Redgrave. I have always wanted to meet Vanessa Redgrave. I think she is brilliant. I saw her in a play in London in 1989. She was brilliant and beautiful playing Isadora. I had thought that of her when she played in Julia, the way she played a character as courageous and fearless and stubborn as I imagine Vanessa Redgrave to be. When Vanessa Redgrave made her

Oscar acceptance speech that year and spoke in support of Palestine she was greater than the character she played.

I worry that Vanessa Redgrave would not want to meet me if she even knew that I existed. I worry I have not done anything as brilliant or beautiful or courageous to warrant her wanting to meet me.

I worry that I am not self absorbed enough to be interesting to others. When I looked at the Annie Liebowitz photo book "Photographs of Her Life 1990-2005" I worried that I had not done anything relevant or interesting nor ever created art or ever been photographed naked while pregnant and that maybe I had made a mistake in never having a baby. I worried that I had never taken a great photograph or ever written a great essay. I worried that I was not as good as everyone in every one of the pictures in the book and that Annie Liebowitz would never take my picture or worse than that –that she would not want to take my picture. I do not worry whether I would want her to take my picture. But I think I would like for her to photograph Woody and me.

I worry that I will never see Kailas again. Kailas was my dog, an English mastiff. She died last August, August 7, 2006. So I never will see her again and that worries me. I worry that I cannot seem to grasp the loss.

# 2

# WHEN I LEARNED I HAD SOMETHING REAL TO WORRY ABOUT

I wrote "Before I Knew What I had To Worry About" a few weeks after my 52nd birthday. My birthday is March 8. I turned 52 in 2007. I just sat down to write out a few thoughts about why I worry and why I still work so many hours doing work that is so stressful. When I am working people's lives are at stake. It seems legitimate and compassionate to worry. I really have been very clever in that I do work that any person would see that worry and concern are appropriate. Even if people do not see worrying as appropriate, people do not see it- the worry- as pathological. For whatever reason it is very important to me not to be seen as pathological, which means I still care very much about what other people think of me and do not spend enough time thinking about what I think about myself. I just worry. And so it went, until Woody's birthday.

Woody is my girlfriend. I have not quite evolved to the language that Woody is my domestic partner, although she is my domestic partner, or will be as soon as we sign the paper in front of the notary public and write out the check for $33.00 and mail the form off to the Secretary of State's Office in Sacramento. I have not yet done that because I worry about what will happen if Woody and I break up. I also worry that the Federal Government is collecting some list of all the domestic partners and then somehow the Federal Government will round us all up and do oppressive things to us, like not allow us to marry and not allow us to file joint income tax returns and disproportionately tax us. They do that already, so I really do not know what I am afraid of. I do not think that it could get worse. But I worry that it might.

I am writing this after Woody's 55th birthday which is roughly 6 weeks after my birthday. And we will be domestic partners on May 15. I like the number 15. I worry that if we do it on a day that is not a good number then our domestic partnership will be doomed. And I do not want to worry about the fate of our relationship because I picked a bad number day to do the domestic partner form filing.

# 3

# WOODY'S BIRTHDAY

**W**oody and I went to the Ritz Carlton in Half Moon Bay California to celebrate her 55th birthday. The Ritz Carlton sits right on the edge of California with the Pacific Ocean to the west and a gorgeous golf course and some luxury houses to the east. It feels affluent yet not pretentious. There are so many workers at the hotel to ask "how are you?" and "may I be of service?" that every guest is made to feel important. Actually they are so good and conscientious that I did not worry at all about anything when we checked in. That was nice.

Woody's birthday is April 21 and this year, 2007, April 21 was on a Saturday. We played golf in the morning. I am not much of a golfer. I can hit the ball really far, which can be a good or a bad thing depending on which direction the ball goes. I have talked on national cable television about golf, but in the context of a criminal trial. It was during the Scott Peterson trial, when the jury was deliberating and all the television "news" stations were on verdict watches and the various cable shows had legal pundits on to speculate about what the jury was doing and what different results would mean. Sometime during one of the shows that I was punditting on the host asked me if I played golf and then asked about the quality of my game. I responded, "On the golf course I have more mood swings than golf swings" and that "I have a lot of mood swings."

I like that description of my golf game. It is accurate. Consequently I worry about playing golf. I worry that I will play badly and then have a meltdown and I worry that I will have an emotional meltdown and then I will play badly. Either way I think the problem is that clearly I worry about what others will think of my golf game. But the more I play the less I seem to worry because I have gotten better.

The Ocean Course at the Ritz is gorgeous. The fairways are long and wide. The grass is perfectly green and inviting. There are very few trees and not a lot of water hazards. It is just wide open and hopeful. Woody shot a 43 on the front 9. She beat me and Gary and Justin. Justin is a second year, soon to be third year law student who works for me. Gary is an Irish carpenter who helped build Woody's studio. Woody beat them both on the second nine as well. This was only fitting as it was Woody's birthday.

Justin and I shared a golf cart and Woody and Gary shared a cart. I think Woody and Gary beat Justin and me. I played pretty well. I did not have a major melt down and did not embarrass myself. I actually enjoyed the scenery and the company and when it was mercifully over it started to rain and I had lost only 5 golf balls. I rated the experience a positive one mainly because for whatever reason I did not worry out on the course. Nothing seemed to matter.

After golf we had lunch together and the fellas went home. Woody and I checked into the hotel. Again everyone asked how we were as we were escorted to a wonderful room with a magnificent view of the ocean and the patio and the eighteenth green of the golf course. It drizzled and was overcast but not foggy so we could see as far as could be seen.

We went for massages in the spa. When we arrived at the spa and checked in we were directed to the locker room where more employees asked if there was anything they could do for us. We were pampered. Woody read a magazine. I took a hot tub and then we each got massages, great massages. We met in the elegant dark showers and showered, changed and returned to our room.

By now it was almost sun set. A bagpiper played under the cover of the gazebo. I opened our window just like all the other guests. We watched the bagpiper play and listened to the bagpipes and the gentle rain and the waves breaking on the rocks. Together it was perfect and beautiful. I felt content and calm. So did Woody. It was really nice, one of those magic times I will remember forever, even though I had forgotten until I just wrote that, about how great it all was. I forgot because I relaxed and I lay on the bed, the huge bed with the 5 million count thread sheets, great sheets, and I felt my right breast.

Just before I felt my right breast I had a thought and a feeling, an experience that something was going to change. That something was going to happen that never again would my life be the same, that never again would anything seem so casual. It was such an odd sensation that I should feel that in my life, whatever it is, nothing would be so enjoyable or innocent or free or something that I still have not been able to define. Just after that experience I felt my right breast. I felt a lump in my right breast on the right side. I knew as soon as I felt the lump/bump it was a very important bump. It was important enough for me to feel. It was important enough for me to notice. It was a very important bump. But I decided not to tell

Woody about the newly discovered important bump because it was her birthday. I did not want her to worry.

Birthdays are important. I believe that on a person's birthday everything should be about the celebrant. So this was Woody's day. I did not want to spoil Woody's day by disclosing that I had just discovered an important lump in my right breast. I do not believe the day after a birthday shares any such protections so I told Woody on Sunday morning.

We had spent a great birthday together. We slept in the five million count sheets. We slept with the windows open and the rain falling and the waves breaking and the cacophony was so peaceful that we slept in late. I felt the lump when I woke up and my lump was still there. That is when I told Woody. We discussed calling Michelle, my doctor and then we were done with the lump. We went about our day as if there was no important lump.

When we got back home after Sunday at the Ritz we were greeted by our dogs. The dogs acted as if we had been gone for weeks although we were gone barely more than 30 hours. Woody has a whippet named Floyd. I have a mastiff named Manaswar. Manaswar was the runt of Kailas' litter. Kailas is the dog who died last year of a combination of old age and a stroke and who I miss so much that I yearn for her. Manaswar looks more like a manatee than a mastiff. She has suffered from behavioral problems. I had to send Manaswar to doggie rehab because she was so aggressive. It was fear-based aggression, but aggression nevertheless. But with Kailas' death Manaswar and I have trauma bonded. We all have become closer. The dogs knew something was up. Our energy was off. They sensed it. They sensed our fear. I called my friend who is girlfriends with my doctor, the gynecologist. I also called the doctor's office. I knew that this was an important lump and that I needed to get in touch with my doctor, Michelle.

9

I had just run into Michelle. I saw her at an AA meeting. She was with a friend of mine. Anonymity is the spiritual foundation of Alcoholics Anonymous and who is at a meeting and what is said at a meeting is supposed to stay at the meeting. I know that. But I am going to break the rule with Michelle's permission. My doctor Michelle Bourgault is not an alcoholic. Michelle was just there at the meeting as a support person. The odd part of the experience was that I walked into the AA meeting, a meeting that I usually attend and have attended for almost twenty years and took the seat that I have sat in for most of the last ten years. I was late. I was dressed up in lawyer clothes. I usually change my clothes because the lawyer clothes, usually Escada, are really quite something and I do not want to stand out at the meeting.

It was a Tuesday night about two months ago. I walked in late to my regular AA meeting very dressed up in Escada. I saw a friend of mine I had not seen in quite a while. Sitting next to her was this woman I knew I knew but could not place. The meeting went on. A few times the woman and I exchanged glances. I smiled and she smiled at me. I still could not place her. I knew I knew her intimately. I knew that I should know her and how I knew her. After the meeting I hugged my friend. My friend asked me if I knew Michelle. I smiled and I said "of course." I pulled Michelle aside and said, "this is embarrassing but I don't remember how I know you." Michelle pulled me even more aside and said she had to tell me in private. Michelle then whispered in my ear, "I am your gynecologist."

How does one politely tell their very own gynecologist that they were not recognized? I am not sure there is any polite way. I said, "I guess I did not recognize you without my knees framing your face". Hardly a polite thing to say, but believably true. Michelle told me that I should come in for a check up. I told her that I had recently included her in a story that I had written. I emailed the story to her. We connected and it was really fun.

So it was Michelle I called that Sunday in every way that I knew to reach her. We did not talk on Sunday. Woody and I watched Desperate Housewives and I fell asleep. Michelle and I spoke on Monday. She set up an appointment for Tuesday morning. That was April 24, 2007.

# 4

# LEARNING ABOUT HOW MUCH THERE IS TO WORRY ABOUT

May 13, 2007

I am not sure how I got from April 21, 2007 to May 13, 2007 but obviously I did. I have worried about so many things over the past few weeks I am not sure whether I can even remember them all. But I want to write all of this down now before I start chemotherapy because I read that one of the possible side effects of chemotherapy is chemo brain, which means my short-term memory may be impaired. So I am writing this now with the imperative of possible impairment.

Since I mentioned chemotherapy then it hardly comes as a surprise that I was diagnosed with cancer. I got the formal diagnosis on

Monday, May 6, 2007. But I knew that the doctors thought I had cancer pretty much from their first contact with me. That was odd. All of the doctors were way ahead of me.

On Monday, April 23, 2007 Dr. Michelle Bourgault returned my call or rather someone from her office called me and arranged an appointment for the following day. Woody and I did not talk much about the important right lump. Mondays used to be my hardest day because I did Drug Court and Proposition 36 Court. Drug Court is a prosecution alternative court and it is really a good idea but it also takes a lot out of me because I want more for the client than to avoid jail. I want them to get "it". I cannot define "it" since a lot of the time I do not have "it.". But I believe "it" is that state when one does not exert energy over things they cannot control. It is a state of acceptance. I do not know who gets to get "it" or who gets to keep "it" as "it" seems to come and go. But I care and there are a lot of people with a lot of problems in Drug Court and it requires me to be completely present. Prop 36 is a state mandated treatment rather than traditional punishment program. Prop 36 tends not to be effective for persons with serious drug problems because they never get to treatment, but that is a whole other story.

Suffice to say Mondays are long and hard for me and I earn relatively little money for the huge amount of work. Since being given a cancer diagnosis I have decided not to do Drug Court anymore. I do not have the energy. There was a deputy district attorney who had done Drug Court for the past few years. His name is Paul Wendler. Paul was diagnosed with pancreatic cancer about a year ago. He did chemotherapy after surgery. Paul died about six months after his diagnosis. Throughout his last months Paul worked in Drug Court. Unlike Paul I knew that I could not continue doing Drug Court. It was sad working in Drug Court without Paul. The thought of doing it now without him and with cancer seemed intolerable.

On Tuesday morning April 24, 2007, I went to court in South San Francisco at the San Mateo County North Courthouse. I found a friend of mine to cover my appearances and I left for the Doctor's office. I was nervous. I hate going to the doctor, any doctor, even when I like the doctor. I always have been reluctant. Who knows why that is, but I am that way.

I saw Michelle at her busy office that Tuesday morning. She did a breast exam. She described my breasts as "challenging". Even though I am small my breasts are not and they are filled with junk. Michelle ordered a mammogram and an ultrasound. She looked worried when she did the exam. She told me to come back to the Hospital at 2:00 p.m., which gave me four hours.

I went to the Federal Prison in Dublin to see a dear friend who unfortunately is now a client in between seeing Michelle and my mammogram. It takes four hours to get back and forth. Four hours is just enough time to get there and get through security, see Greg and get back. I do not like going. Prisons are not fun. Seeing people in prison is not fun. But the prison offered a refuge from everyone so that no one except Greg could see how worried I was about the mammogram. I hate mammograms. They hurt and they are uncomfortable.

I went back to St. Luke's Hospital in San Francisco. I went to the Breast Center. They did a mammogram. They squeezed my breasts and flattened them. They did each breast. I remembered why I hate mammograms. They hurt and they are uncomfortable.

My left nipple is pierced. I pierced it when I turned 46 so that when I was in court and everything was going to shit I could think to myself "ha-ha my nipple is pierced". I have been treated for post traumatic stress, substance abuse and depression and even after tons of therapy and treatment that is what I came up with to feel good about myself-pierce my left nipple. My left nipple hurt at the beginning of April. It had never hurt before. The ring felt stuck. So I twisted the ring and rubbed cream on it and forgot about it.

I had not remembered that my left nipple had hurt me until after the cancer diagnosis. The breast center mammogrammed my right breast first because that is where the suspicious lump was. Then they did my left breast. I then left the mammogram room. After a few minutes they came and got me and remammogrammed my left breast. They squished it and photographed it and squished it and photographed and then asked questions.

Then came the ultrasound. The radiologist Dr. Dulcy Woolverton was kind and friendly but I knew by the look on her face that something was bothering her. I just hoped it was not my right breast.

She did my right breast first. She showed me the bump and explained that the bump was a cyst and was no cause for alarm. I was ready to go then. I was so relieved that she was not concerned with my right breast that I had completely forgotten about my left breast. Dulcy continued the ultrasound this time showing me my left breast. She still looked worried. That made no sense to me as my right breast was okay. I had never thought about my left breast. I knew as soon as she started that I should have been more careful in my requests in that I had only asked for a reprieve regarding my right breast. Dulcy showed me the tumor in my left breast. I knew by the look on her face that the core needle biopsy that she would schedule would confirm her belief that I have a cancerous tumor in my left breast.

I had the core needle biopsy the following day. Dulcy stayed late to do the procedure. Michelle arranged for me to meet Dr. Lora Burke the day of the bad mammogram and confirmatory ultrasound. Dr. Burke seemed great. She confirmed my initial impression because she came down and helped Dulcy with the biopsy. Dulcy wore a tiara because her birthday was the next day. I took an Ativan before the procedure. I babbled and blabbed through the whole thing. I kept my eyes shut after I saw the instrument. It looks like a meat thermometer. It hurt. But I knew from Dulcy's face and Lora's face that I had a cancerous tumor. As it turned out I do have a cancerous tumor. They were right. And the discovery of the cancer in my left breast was because of my right breast. Clearly after my left breast had hurt and I had essentially ignored the pain in my left beast what choice did my body have other than to make a cyst in my right breast. It was during the biopsy that I explained the right breast cyst phenomena as my right breast saying, "Help! Help! Lefty's in trouble and she can't speak." Righty did a good job for Lefty.

I did not need the pathology results to tell me. I knew that I had a cancerous tumor in my left breast. I knew from the look on Dulcy's face. I knew from the look on Dr. Burke's face. I knew by the look on her face when she did the initial exam that there was a cancerous tumor in my left breast. The pathology report confirmed my suspicions. What I did not know was that there are different types of tumors. Breast tumors are different in terms of size and shape (differentiation) as well as what feeds the tumor. My tumor is about 3 centimeters long, yet narrow, and grossly differentiated. My tumor is estrogen positive, progesterone positive, and HER2 positive. That essentially means that everything makes my tumor grow.

I did not know what any of that meant. I was warned to stay off the internet because there is a lot of misinformation as well as out of context information as well as good information. The problem is I do not know enough to differentiate and discern. So I read some books. Then I decided to write one. I would rather think about my life and what to do than learn the science of cancer. As it turns out I have done both.

# 5

# STEROIDS MAKE SOME PEOPLE TURN RED

This is the third day since my first chemotherapy session. It has been terrible. The Tuesday chemo was not really that bad. But most everything that has followed has been bad. I did not realize that before they administer chemo drugs they first give steroids. Apparently steroids do something to quash nausea. They gave me 20 mgs. of some steroid called dexasomething. After the chemotherapy I did not have much nausea. Instead I had an allergic reaction to the steroids that I am still having as I type.

My reaction to the steroids manifests as swelling. I am so swollen. My reaction manifests as redness in my skin. By Thursday when I was to enter Avenal State Prison I was beet red and swollen. I looked like Hitch, the movie character, a red version of Will Smith's Hitch. If you did not see the movie then I looked like a red version of the

Michelin man. I looked bad and felt worse. I drove to Avenal Prison. I was accompanied by a young man, actually not so young, 34 year old man, who is licensed to practice law in Pennsylvania and not in California. His name is Kelton. I drove. I had no business driving. For most of the drive I did nothing more than swell and occasionally yell at an answering machine of a medical office that I called to complain that I was swelling. I only got answering machines or services because it was early as we drove because our appointment at the prison was for 10 a.m.

So I drove and I yelled and I swelled and then we got to the prison. We went to the reception area of the prison in the administration building. I have been there four times at least before this trip. I know the routine. The visitor has to check in with the receptionist. The receptionist in turn calls the Legal Affairs Office and the Legal Affairs Secretary sometimes comes out or the Legal Affairs Officer comes out. On this particular day the Secretary came out. She looked at Kelton and then she looked at me and then she said, "I was not expecting two of you. I thought only Mr. B. (aka Kelton) was coming. The woman continued, "Only Mr. B. is authorized to see Mr. X. You may not see him because there was no request." I said, "oh really," and glared at Kelton. I was getting redder.

I explained to the Legal Affairs Secretary at the Avenal State Prison in Avenal California, some 200 miles south of San Francisco and some 300 miles north of Los Angeles and out in the middle of absolutely nowhere, that Kelton worked for me and that his job was not to arrange a visit for himself. Rather his job was to arrange my visit and he would accompany me. She asked me to keep my voice down. I was still getting redder. I was also still swelling but the redness was far more striking than the swelling. I asked Kelton to show me the letter that he had sent arranging the visit. I showed the letter to the Legal Affairs Secretary. The letter was written on my letterhead, meaning my name appears prominently at the top of the paper i.e. Law Offices of Paula Canny, address, telephone numbers etc. I showed the woman the letter.

I pointed to the letterhead and I said "this person is me and he (referring to Kelton) works for me but he will not work for me, meaning I will fire him on the spot if because of this letter I am not able to see my client. Not only will I fire him I will leave him here because I will not let him back in my car." I meant it. The Legal Affairs Secretary was starting to get red. She asked me again to keep my voice down. There was an African-American man waiting across the lobby for an interview. The Legal Affairs Secretary told me that my anger was making him uncomfortable. I found it fairly remarkable that this woman who was not going to let me see my client was so sensitive to a job applicant's apparent discomfort over my anger. I sensed that the applicant was uncomfortable but I speculated that he thought the woman's position was unreasonable.

It was clear that Kelton works for me. It was clear the inmate was my client. It was clear that if there was a mistake Kelton had made it. It was also clear that I had been in the prison to see the inmate on at least four prior occasions and had been there as recently as two months ago. The woman again informed me that only Mr. B. could see the inmate.

I tried to reason with her. I was getting redder and I am sure that the woman thought I was having an absolute biological reaction to her assertion of authority. Kelton was red as well. He had started to sweat. My ears were red. His ears turned red as the Legal Affairs Secretary continued to tell me that it was impossible for me to see my client because Kelton had notified them that only he was coming.

The lady and I exchanged proposed solutions. Her solution was to have Kelton see the inmate and I could just wait for him. My solution was that I see the inmate and Kelton could wait for me. She repeated that only Kelton had prior authorization. I tried to reason that Kelton could not discuss that which I was there to discuss otherwise I would have just sent Kelton. She did not seem movable. When we exchanged the same unacceptable solutions a few times I proposed a third solution and that was that no one see the inmate now and that I would simply make another appointment. I would return next week. I then looked at her in the eyes and said, "I am going to lose my hair next week and I had wanted to see my client before I go bald. And I am going to lose my hair because I was just diagnosed with breast cancer and I have just begun chemotherapy and I am not having a good week so you can either let me see him today or I will be back next week even angrier and very bald so you take your pick, let me see him today or I come back next week completely bald and even angrier." She let me see my client that day.

And as worried as she was about my return and having to deal with me again, I am more worried about what it will be like to be bald. Clearly the thought of going bald as well as the thought of being bald is freaking me out. I do not want to lose my hair. I do not want to be like everyone else who does the kind of chemo treatment that I am doing. I do not want anyone who sees me unless I have an incredible wig to know that I have cancer. That is why I tell people I have cancer and have started chemotherapy. I want to feel like I have some power whether people know or not. Once I am bald people will either think that I am doing chemo, that I have alopecia or to some extreme people that I have a Britney Spears obsession. I do not really like any of those options. I do not want to be sick. Even more, I do not want people to know that I am sick.

It all comes back to the fact that I worry about what people think about me. And again that is so silly because what other people think about me is really none of my business. Nevertheless, knowing that fact does not stop my worrying both about what other people think as well as worrying about what other people think about me. I have to let go of my attachment to others' opinions. It is odd. This concern about what others think of me does not apply to everyone. I worry about people who I do not even know who they are- I worry about what they think. As to specific people, I do not necessarily care. It depends on the person. I really did not care what the Legal Affairs Secretary thought of me. Yet that might not even be true. I knew even then I did not want the Legal Affairs Secretary to see me bald. I guess I do care.

Once it was agreed that we could both see the client Kelton and I were escorted by a prison guard back through the entrance to the prison itself. The administration building is outside of the walled-in prison area. We went through checkpoints and gates and metal detectors and at about the last possible point the guards discovered Kelton's cell phone. That cell phone happens to be the very same cell phone that I had said I thought ought to be left in the car as prisons do not allow cell phones. At the car I did not make an issue of it. This was of course before the whole admissions fiasco. The guards would not let us in the prison because of the cell phone. The guards would not hold it at the desk. Kelton's solution was to leave it on the ground outside the security unit and he would pick it up on the way out of the prison. I reminded Kelton that we were in a prison and that I doubted that a Blackberry cell phone would be left alone on the ground for several hours.

I took his Blackberry cell phone and returned to the car and left it there. It was a long walk of about a quarter of a mile. I took my time. I felt terrible and kind of dizzy and oddly out of my red swollen body as if the liquid was pushing me out. Perhaps that is where the expression being "out of it" comes from. I was out of it, the "it" being my body- me. So, out of my body I returned to the security building in the prison. Kelton and I were escorted again through all of the very same security precautions that we had initially done before the discovery of Kelton's cell phone. It was no more fun the second time than the first. I was continuing to swell. I could not get much redder.

We got to the visiting office. I had brought a fleece jacket to wear in the office because they keep the visiting rooms so cold. I mean really cold. I kind of think it is done on purpose so that the visits are not very long just because a person could freeze in the room. I always take a fleece or something warm anytime I visit a prison.

We waited for over an hour before my client arrived. I did not say much to Kelton other than occasionally saying to him phrases like "what the fuck were you thinking" and "how could you have neglected to mention that the purpose of the visit was for me to see the client". Kelton did not say too much. My client was searched before he came in to the room. He did not have anything other than his cane. He is elderly and frail. He has a long white beard and he looks like Santa Claus. We greeted each other with hugs.

The first words out of his mouth were, "I have been praying for you. Kelton told me about your cancer." As bad as my day was, and it was bad from the swelling and the redness and the overall body discomfort, I was fairly certain that Kelton's day was worse. I did not tell Kelton to tell my client I had cancer. I am fairly certain that I had said just the opposite and that is not to tell him. Kelton knew that. I knew that Kelton knew that and now wondered if the letter fiasco was not a mistake. I actually was fairly calm. But when Kelton cut his finger getting a file out of the file box on a staple that he had left in a file I really was pleased. I looked at him as he was bleeding and said, "It is still not enough".

We did our business, which was very interesting and very privileged which is why I have not written the client's name or discussed the nature of my work. We exchanged hugs and we were off.

By the time I got back to the car I was bigger and redder. I felt really bad. I told Kelton that the only reason I was letting him get in the car was because I might need him to call an ambulance or something on the way home. If I was healthy I would have left him. Insanely, I would not let Kelton drive saying I did not trust him. I really barely remember the ride home other than the wig lady called and made an appointment for me to see her and get a wig the following week. Just past Coalinga where the cow slaughter yard is I vowed to not eat meat. Acres and acres of hundreds and hundreds of cows making a giant stench made me sick.

Cows by the way were meant to eat grass. There is no grass in the slaughterhouse yards. There are troughs of cornmeal. Cows are not meant to eat corn and there is something in corn even before the giant US agriculture industry started to genetically alter the corn that causes or contributes to cancer cell growth. So cows eat corn that they should not eat and that they were not meant to eat because people give the cows corn instead of grass. People give the cows corn because it is cheaper and hence more profitable to feed cows cheap corn on dirty cow manure filled dirt lots than let the cows roam the range and graze on grass.

The sad part is I like the taste of hamburger, steak, prime rib and all that meat stuff. I just cannot think that I am eating a cow, much less a Coalinga cow. And I am losing my hair soon and there will be no more beef and so far the only thing I have gotten from the cancer experience is red and swollen. But I may save a few cows along the way.

I stayed red for few more days. I stayed swollen for a few more days. One of the nurses suggested swimming. Without realizing how difficult it would be Woody and I flew to Southern California with my 86 year old mother to go to my brother's graduation from law school. But the hotel had the hottest swimming pool, almost hot tub hot pool water that was perfect for me. So I swam and swam and somehow the water evened me out and then the water in me eventually left me. Due to my then unknown now very known steroid allergy I gained and lost 14 pounds in water in four days. That did not feel good. That was worse than being red.

# 6

# WORRYING ABOUT ROUND TWO OF CHEMO

The doctor agreed that he would not give me steroids for the next round. We could try it without steroids, but he warned me about nausea. Brad-Dr. Ekstrand-the oncologist measured the tumor when he first saw me. At this visit he measured the tumor again. He said he believes that the tumor is already shrinking some. He measured the tumor as being less than 2.5 centimeters down from 3. That is great and precisely the reason I chose to do the chemo on the front end of treatment. So that I could know that the chemo poison was actually poisoning the cancer. That makes me very happy.

But my left breast feels weird. I am not sure if it is real or imagined but I believe there might be a war going on in my left breast.

It is ironic that there is a war going on in my left breast. I am a pacifist. I think I am except as it relates to cancer. I want to kill the cancer. I hope that I want to kill the cancer more than the cancer wants to kill me, if cancer even knows that it is killing. Cancer might just be trying to live, more and more, living large, maybe that is all that cancer wants. Cancer apparently wants to live large in my left breast, which is not that large. But it is big enough to be home to an invasive 3 centimeter cancer thing. So the chemo is fighting the cancer and I think that the cancer is trying to kill the chemo and all that is going on in my left breast.

I wonder if Iraq is like my left breast, or rather I wonder if my left breast is like Iraq, a huge civil war. Mine is on a cellular level. Nevertheless, it is a war. My left breast was invaded several years ago. I pierced my left nipple on my 46th birthday. I went to a piercing studio with Sarah and I pierced my left nipple. It really hurt. I had worn a steel ring with a small onyx bead until about one month ago. After the core needle biopsy I took the ring out of my nipple. I still had the nipple ring when I had the first mammogram and the ultrasound. The picture of the mammogram distinctly shows the nipple ring. Consequently it made it hard for me to argue that the cancer in the mammogram was not my breast. It was clear from the first picture that there was cancer in the breast with the nipple ring.

I really do not think that the piercing of my left nipple led to the cancer war in my left breast. When I draw the comparison to my left breast and Iraq I was trying to draw some parallel to the fact that Iraq was invaded and perhaps the piercing is like the United States invasion of Iraq. Maybe Iraqis feel that the United States' invasion of their country is cancerous. Maybe the United States invaded Iraq because they thought the U.S. invasion is the cure, kind of like chemotherapy. It all does come down to one's perspective.

The chemotherapy seems to be winning the war in my left breast. When I saw my oncologist last week he re-measured the cancer in my left breast and said that the growth appears to have shrunk to under 2.5 centimeters. That is good. That is shrinkage by .5 centimeters. If there is shrinkage of .5 after every chemo treatment that means there will be no cancer left after 6 treatments. I hope that is true, and that the last two treatments are the icing on the cake so to speak.

I have another chemo treatment tomorrow. Today I am a bit grumpy which is perhaps why there is the War metaphor contained herein. It is also Memorial Day Weekend and there is a war raging in Iraq. I think my cancer and really all cancer is a solvable problem. It is simply a matter of time and resource allocation. The war in Iraq is not solvable. The budget for the United States government as proposed by President Bush allocates one billion dollars a day towards the war in Iraq. The cancer research amount in his proposed budget contains a 500 million dollar reduction from the 2007 budget from 6 billion to 5.5 billion dollars. So President Bush proposes spending five and a half days of war on cancer research. Crazy. Absolutely crazy. And I can only wonder what a different place this world would be if George W. Bush's father would have gotten cancer instead of being dissed by Sadam Huissein. We could have had a war on cancer. It is a war that could be won in the President's lifetime. Instead we are in a war that will be lost and we continue to lose not just the war but every other thing that the war money could be spent upon, whether it is cancer research, Aids research, education, or even food. My war in my left breast will be over before the war in Iraq is over. I have a far better chance of winning my left breast war than we do the war in Iraq.

Maybe the only thing to do is give everyone in Iraq, or everyone fighting in Iraq chemotherapy. Then they will be too sick to fight and the war will be over. I am scared about chemo. I am afraid that I will get sick because I will not get steroids anymore because of my prior allergic reaction. One chemo infusion down seven to go. I have to believe that I can do this. I can. Tons of people have gone through this and far worse than this. I can do this. But I do not want just to do this. I want the chemo to work. I want to win. I do not want to have cancer.

A lot of people I know who have had cancer have died of cancer. That happens. It does not happen as much as it used to. But still it happens. I do not want to die from cancer. I will die of something. There could be far worse things than dying of cancer, like dying in a car bomb in Iraq, or being kidnapped by a Muslim fanatic and then shot in some terrible hostage drama, like Daniel Pearl, or being blown up by a roadside bomb while riding in a humvee like some thousands of American soldiers, or starving to death in Darfur, or being stoned to death in Pakistan for simply being a woman rape victim. So maybe dying from cancer is not so bad relatively. I am not dying now. I am just trying to live through chemotherapy.

# 7

# ROUND TWO

I did my second chemotherapy on May 29, 2007. This time I was not given any steroids. I got there at twelve thirty. Marta was already there. Marta is my friend. Marta is a Judge. Marta is great, a great judge and a better person. Marta tells me to be nice to Woody. Sometimes I need to be told the obvious. I did not yell at Woody at all that morning. I walked Manaswar on the beach. I then went to the gym, worked out and then came home. We had eggs over easy with raisin toast. I showered and put on my chemo outfit including underwear, fairly nice conservative underwear because, after all, it is a doctor's office. Ever since I was a little girl my mother warned me about the dangers of wearing ratty underwear. If I wore ratty underwear a doctor might see my ratty underwear, and then I would be shamed by my bad underwear. Worse yet the doctor would be appalled by my bad underwear and then somehow offer inferior treatment to me because of my bad underwear.

Rather than test the truth of any of those propositions I choose to wear decent conservative respectful underwear any time I go to any doctor's office. So I wore decent underwear that no one saw yesterday underneath my chemo outfit. My chemo outfit is a t-shirt, white short sleeves that over the chest just above the heart has the letter T imprinted. The T stands for trust and on one of the sleeves the word trust is written. I got that t-shirt at my meditation ashram a few years ago, when the message was Trust. That is a good message and I do trust. I trust my doctors, nurses, my friends, and most of all God, although I am not sure what God is, or who God is. I do know that I am not God. I trust the power that gives life in all its forms as well as changes the form of life, and I call that power God, only because I have no other name.

I have had a varied religious experience in my life. I went to small Catholic girls schools for most of my education. I went to Saint Anthony's and then Marymount in Arlington, Virginia. I actually started school outside London in Pinner, England at Woodridings School. Woodridings is an English school and I was the only American. I think I liked it. We wore uniforms. I wore a brown jumper with a white shirt, brown shoes and an orange tie and good underwear.

My favorite Woodridings story is about my performance or lack thereof at the May Day Games, a kind of elementary school mini Olympics. There were running races and sack races and three leg races and the big event was the Easter egg pick up. In that event each child is given an Easter basket and assigned an egg color. The task is to run approximately forty yards and to pick up the designated color Easter egg at intervals along the way and put the egg in the basket. The goal is to be the first to cross the finish line carrying all the picked up eggs in the basket.

When I did the event I was fast, very fast. Even young I was fast and even young I was determined. I was given my basket and a designated egg color. Now I cannot remember the color. I stood at the start line with my classmates, now competition, and I mustered all my American competitive spirit and decided I would be the first to cross the finish line. I actually was the first to cross the finish line. But I was not the winner. My problem was that every time I ran and picked up an egg and put it in my basket, it bounced out because I was running so wildly. I crossed the finish line first, far ahead of any of my competition only to discover I was eggless. I was very disappointed.

I returned to the course to retrieve my fallen eggs. I did get them all and again crossed the finish line. But this time I was last.

I did not learn a lot from that experience as I have continued to move so quickly that often times I miss the point of an exercise. But I like that story. I did learn to curtsy at Woodridings. I had to learn. I was selected to give the Headmistress a bouquet of flowers at the May Day celebration. Just prior to presenting the Headmistress with the bouquet I was required to curtsy. I did as instructed. I still can curtsy, but I still have trouble keeping my eggs in a basket so to speak.

After I did a fine curtsy and presented the Headmistress with the bouquet she thanked me and also made a joke about how Americans cannot keep their eggs in their baskets. Everyone laughed. I may have smiled. I may have felt like crying. That probably would have been appropriate, but really I felt anger. I hated the baskets, the eggs, the stupid rule requiring all the eggs to be in the basket to qualify to win. It could have been at that time that I started to think about becoming a lawyer.

When my family returned to the United States my mother put me in Catholic schools. The first was a parochial school called Saint

Anthony's. At Saint Anthony's in a two year period I did my first Confession, first Holy Communion, and Confirmation. And it was at Saint Anthony's that the seeds of resentment were planted that grew into my absolute rejection of Catholicism in particular and organized religion in general. That resentment served to torture me for the next twenty years. I have worked all of that out, or rather a lot of it out so that now my chemo outfit consists of the trust t-shirt that symbolizes trust in God. Now I do.

I also trust in God's gifts, in people and things. Some of God's people and my friends brought me one of God's creations last night to help with the terrible nausea I have. God's gift was marijuana, ripe, pungent and powerful marijuana. But I did not smoke any of it because I passed out. But I like knowing that I have options other than pills like lorazapam or Ativan that totally knock me out.

# 8

# THREE DAYS AFTER THE SECOND INFUSION

It is three days later. I am now in boxer shorts. I sleep in boxer shorts. There is no need to worry about doctors or respectful underwear. I have just finished just about the worst three days of my life. June 1, 2007. Another month, I have made it through the end of April and the entire month of May. I have my last chemotherapy treatment on August 21, 2007. And I will never do chemotherapy again. At least right now I say so. But this is bad, seriously bad.

Getting the chemo is not that bad. I go to the Hope Infusion Center, which I have not written about before. I have said it many times to my friends; they should call it the Auschwitz Infusion Center. That is the truth of it. Poison-medicinal poison-that is what chemotherapy is. I knew chemotherapy was bad. I have watched others get chemotherapy. I have written wills for people on their deathbed from cancer and chemotherapy. I knew it was difficult on people in so many ways. I have watched people suck on ice to diminish the nausea and quench what is a relentless thirst tempered by perpetual nausea.

I let them give me Ativan intravenously before the chemo and that makes me relaxed and very high. I take a pill called emend before the chemotherapy. The pill costs $150.00 a pill. It is a strong pill and it is supposed to be taken in conjunction with the dexa steroid that I am allergic to and was not given this time. The difference in not getting the steroid is huge. I am not red. I am not swollen. I am not running around with all that crazy energy and not in my body when I am doing any of it. But I am also nauseous. I did not take the third day of emend because when I took it the second day it made me homicidal. I was happy and then I took the pill and my whole mood changed to anger. That is bad. So I did not take the third day of emend and my nausea was really bad.

I have had really bad nausea before. In 1991 I climbed Mount Kilimanjaro. We took the Shira Route. The Shira Route is the back way and the long way to the summit. That route allows one to see the glacier and walk on the glacier. That is the glacier that surrounded the summit of Kilimanjaro that has almost melted away. So I am a very lucky person to have seen the glacier that has melted away in 16 years. I think that glacier had been there for about a million years. And in 16 years it is almost gone. No wonder so many people have cancer. If global warming can alter the earth's temperature so drastically that a million year old glacier can melt away in 16 years why wouldn't a healthy 52 year old woman get breast cancer. It makes sense. I actually think it is worse that the glacier is almost gone than my having cancer. I wish the glacier was not melting away. I wish that I did not have cancer. The cancer may be killed but there is no saving the glacier. That is really sad.

It takes about 5 days to get to the top of Kilimanjaro hiking the Shira Route. I went on an organized trek with a company called Wilderness Travel. Our group leader was an Englishman named Ross Battersby. We had some Kenyan porters and kitchen staff and there were 10 of us in the group. The first night we camped at 12,000 feet. The second camp was at about 14,000 feet. I was strong then. I am still strong but I was 16 years younger and I was in good shape although I smoked cigarettes then.

I paid extra to have my own tent. I loved having my own tent. I loved my privacy. The first camp night after dinner I went to my tent and got in my sleeping bag and listened to a tape of a mantra and read a book called Where Am I Going by Swami Muktananda. It was bliss. I felt very peaceful and committed to climbing Kilimanjaro. Even that has a backstory.

When I was in college I had a boyfriend named Tom. Tom and I each did a junior year abroad. I went to England. Tom went to Kenya and attended the University of Nairobi. On his spring break Tom and some fellow students climbed Mount Kilimanjaro, though they went the tourist route, the front side of the mountain, which means they did not get to experience the glacier that in a year or two will no longer exist so that no one will experience it. But Tom made it to the top.

During our senior year in college any time Tom would have a few drinks and a new audience he would talk about how great it was to have climbed Kilimanjaro. Clearly I got a resentment. Tom would talk about how when he got to the top of the mountain there was a chest. In the chest was a book. And every one who climbs to the top of Kilimanjaro is supposed to write their name in the book that is in the chest. Tom had written his name in the book. Sometime after we had broken up I formulated a plan that I would go and climb Kilimanjaro and erase Tom's name from the book.

So some 16 years after the beginning of my resentment I set off to climb Kilimanjaro. I never really intended to erase Tom's name. I just liked the thought of it. I liked the thought of it because my time in London included an experience that I wish I could erase. I mentioned I was raped four days before I turned 21 and it was terrible. Not as terrible as cancer or maybe it was that terrible and the passage of time has diminished the terror I experienced and the shame of it all. Every time Tom spoke about climbing Kilimanjaro I thought of being raped in London four days before I turned 21 by a fat middle aged Arab man who tricked me, drugged me, kidnapped me and fucked me and then left me.

In the beginning I was proud of Tom for having done such a great adventure. But the more I heard about his great accomplishment and the more I did not heal from the rape the greater my resentment became to the point that Tom and I broke up and I eventually formulated a plan to climb Kilimanjaro and erase his name. When I got to the top of Kilimanjaro there was a chest. In the chest was a book. I signed my name. I did not erase Tom's name. Actually the book I signed was a different book because as the book is filled a new book is placed in the chest and the old books are kept in park headquarters. I could have looked at Tom's book at Park Headquarters and saved myself the trip up. But once I had climbed the mountain my resentment was gone. Ironically I finally understood why Tom regaled others with his story of climbing Kilimanjaro. Climbing Kilimanjaro is by far one of my favorite things I have done in my life.

But at the second camp at 14,000 feet that is not what I thought. I had nausea. I had cramping. I had vomiting. I had diarrhea. I did not have the luxury of a private toilet or bathroom. I did have the luxury of a private rock about 40 feet above my private tent. All night long I spent behind that rock alternating between shivering and sweating and puking and shitting. I would look out over the plains and then off to the mountain top as it was almost a full moon in between gastrointestinal episodes and wonder what I was going to do. I did not want to die out there. I did not want to spend a day out there and then go back. I did not want to go back. I laughed at myself at the folly of my resentment and how funny it would be if I died trying to climb Kilimanjaro to erase Tom's name because I got raped in London. I knew in all that I was insane. I laughed. I cried, I prayed. All the while I sweated. Ross Battersby came up to my rock-almost- a few times to check on me. There was not a lot he could do. I either had intense altitude sickness or dysentery or a combination thereof.

That is what the past few days have been like, except that I have not had diarrhea, nor have I vomited. And I have not been behind a rock but in my bedroom. But I felt constantly nauseous for almost 48 hours. I have sipped about 12 bottles of water, not eaten very much. I have cried, prayed, moaned, prayed, laughed, and prayed some more.

At the second camp at 14,000 feet I was sick all night. At about 5 a.m. I left the rock. I went to my tent and slept for a few hours. I then got up and hiked. I willed myself up that mountain. I drank water and I walked and I willed myself to the very top some 19,000 feet. I feel better now than I did, but I still do not feel well. August 21 is my last chemo treatment and it feels like 19,000 feet.

Somewhere in the misery of the last few days I went to the hair stylist who styled my wig. His name is James. He is in Sausalito and he is great. James was positive and optimistic and gentle. Yet I still do not like my wig. Today my hair started coming out. That is bad, both psychologically and physically. It is has a huge potential for messy. I do not like messy.

My friend Joan came over this morning just as I was discovering that my hair was coming out. Woody still has a virus and does not feel well. We talked about what to do. We went to the local Pacifica barbershop, a genuine barbershop. It is a genuine barbershop because it has a genuine barbershop pole. There are two barbers in the shop Frank and Glenn. Glenn has been there 51 years, and is a character as is Frank. We videotaped the events. Frank told off color jokes. We all had a good laugh. Now I look like a marine. Glenn would not shave me bald but my hair is short, shorter than it has ever been. It does not look that bad. I am so grateful to have any hair at all that I love it. I am afraid of being bald, of having some soft white head. Bald just feels so vulnerable. At least now I am kind of butch. Except that I am not. It is really pretty remarkable, the more hair I have cut off the softer my face has become. I am pretty. My head is pretty. It is really kind of nice.

But this cancer is bad. The treatment is terrible. In a few days I will be bald and every day that I have hair is one less day that I will be bald. For whatever reason that is very important to me.

Also I have learned about a concept called anticipatory nausea. Anticipatory nausea is just what it describes -nausea created just by the thought of the event that causes nausea. I am worrying that I have that now. I have this weird memory of the taste of the Ativan or maybe it is the taste of the chemo and the memory of the taste makes me sick. That worries me because I have six more treatments to go. Four of the last six will require some steroids to fight the reaction to the Taxol. So I feel sick right now.

I like Coca-Cola. One time when I was in the Everest region of Nepal on a trek for no other reason than I wanted to see Mount Everest I was unbelievably sick from a combination of altitude sickness and dysentery. I had climbed Kala Patar. We left our campsite at about 3 a.m. We walked several miles to Gorak Shep where there was only one small teahouse. This was about 13 years ago and there are a lot more than teahouses at Gorak Shep now. I was with a few other trekkers. I was the only woman. We had several Sherpas to help us.

We walked and walked and walked and got to Gorak Shep. It was daybreak. We had some tea and then we climbed and climbed and climbed until we got to the top of Kala Patar where we had the most amazing view of Everest. We stayed on the top of Kala Patar for about a half an hour. We had some crackers that I could barely eat. We took pictures of each other with Everest in the background.

The way down took half of the time as the way up. But by the time I had descended from about 18,500 to 16,500 feet I had a full blown altitude headache as well as the accompanying nausea. When we got to the teahouse at Gorak Shep someone gave me a Power Bar and insisted that I eat it. I tried to eat it. It tasted like saw dust. I said I felt sick. One of the Sherpas, who was carrying oxygen insisted that I have some oxygen. I breathed in the oxygen wearing the oxygen mask. About a minute later I started throwing up like I did when I was at the 14,000 feet camp on the way to the top of Kilimanjaro.

I walked and puked for the next five hours until we got back to our campsite. I felt terrible. When I got back I collapsed in my private tent that I again paid extra to have. The leader Frances Klatzel brought me a Coca-Cola. It was the best thing I have ever tasted. So now whenever I trek I carry a can of Coca-Cola in my daypack. Just knowing it is in my pack makes me feel better. I have a can of Coke next to me right now. And I keep saying to myself that if I could make it through those experiences I can do this.

# 9

# HAIR TODAY GONE TOMORROW

I still have some hair in the form of my GI Jane hair cut. I am obsessed with my hair and the fact that I am losing it. I have not washed my hair because I am fairly sure that when I do it will fall out, or rather wash out but it will be clean. I have decided that I would rather have dirty short hair on my head than clean hair in my drain. I know that I will lose my hair. Everyone who does the chemotherapy protocol that I am doing loses their hair. Nevertheless I want to be the one person who does not lose their hair. I also want to be the person that succeeds in having the chemo kick the cancer's ass, leading me to wonder if cancerous growths have asses. But whatever it has or is I want the chemo to kill it, kind of that impassioned fervor I got as a teenager when I would get a bad zit and I would want to just squeeze it out of existence. I want the chemo to chemo the cancer out of existence and yet I also do not want to go bald.

I look at my short hair. I like my short hair, all of it, and any of it. It is dark brown and there is no color left of all of the colorings I have put into my hair. It is just short dark GI Jane hair. I sang the Halls of Montazuma to Woody yesterday and marched. She was impressed that I knew so many of the words. That is what one gets when they swim for Fort Myer Swim Team for some ten years as Fort Myer is the home of the Iwo Jima Memorial. But not all the singing in the world is going to keep my hair on my head.

Nothing is going to save my hair in the short run. Everyone will see me bald unless I wear a wig that was very expensive. I am not sure there is such a thing as a good wig. Everyone will still know that I am bald. They will also know that I am ashamed about being bald because I am wearing a wig. But the truth is I am ashamed about wearing the wig because I am ashamed that I am bald because apparently I am ashamed that I have cancer. But I prefer not to think about having cancer. I prefer to perseverate about losing my hair.

My hair that I have cut and colored for most of my adult life will come back or so they say. I know I should have an attitude of gratitude. I will try to be grateful. I am grateful for my hair and for all of the years that it has been with me in one form or another. I will save money on my hair since I will not have any for while. I suppose I should also be grateful for the fact that I could do whatever I wanted to my hair.

I have spent a lot of money on my hair over the years. I had a great hairdresser, why they call them hairdressers I do not know. I think hairdressers prefer to be called stylists. I actually call the person who does my hair "the person who does my hair." Susan did my hair for the past few years. But she bought a 40 foot sailboat and sailed with her girlfriend first to Mexico and now is on her way to Tahiti. Susan has not cut my hair for awhile. Susan did a great job on my hair. I miss Susan. I worry about Susan and Elba in their sailboat in the middle of the ocean on their way to Tahiti. I hope they are okay and will soon arrive safely. If Susan were here I would have let Susan shave my head. I trust her and know that it would be okay.

Susan shaved my friend Saundra's head when Saundra had to shave her head because she had a brain tumor and had to have surgery to remove the tumor. I helped Susan shave Saundra's head because Susan had broken her arm and was in a sling. I think she had broken her arm snowboarding but I am not sure. But even with a broken arm Susan was better with the shaver than I was. Susan shaved Saundra's head and then she shaved Saundra's brother's head and a few others of Saundra's friends' heads. It was a fun head shaving party. I have not wanted to have such a party because I still do not want to accept that I am losing my hair. I am busy trying not to lose it.

Over the past few years I have gotten my hair done by the person who does my hair about every two months. That means about six times a year I have my hair done. Having my hair done takes about three hours plus an hour travel time. I have it colored, highlighted and low lighted, washed, conditioned, and then cut. The cost is about $225.00 then another 20 percent more for tip, $20.00 for parking winding up to be roughly $285.00 six times a year for about $1710.00 per year on my hair. I have been spending that much for at least the past 15 years. That totals $25,650.00 over the last 15 years. That is a lot of money. I could have bought two Hyundais for what I have spent on my hair. I had no idea I spent so much. No wonder I am worried about losing my hair. It is not just hair it is a major capital investment.

In terms of my life my hair has taken up tons of time in my life. Now that is an interesting concept. The relationship between time spent on my hair and time spent on my life. My hair has taken up a lot of my money and my time. I spend at least 30 minutes a day washing my hair, meaning I spend roughly 182.5 hours a year taking care of my hair, and that does not include the roughly four hours it takes to go get my hair done and get my hair done roughly six times a year. So I spend about 205 hours a year on my hair. That is four workweeks. I could take a month long vacation by being bald.

I should not be worrying about going bald I should be worrying about what I am going to do with all the extra time I am going to have over the next few months since I will not have any hair. So far I am spending my hair care time worrying about what I will do without any hair. This hair perseveration is an indication that I am not well.

But hair plays a big part in American lives. I think it always has. Think back to the authors of the Declaration of Independence and the Constitution. These great men worried about their hair so much so that many wore wigs. Lawyers in England called barristers still wear wigs. That is not the case in American courts, unless some how I popularize the trend. But I cannot get my wig on today so I am not going to court. My hair, what is left of it hurts as does my tender white scalp. I cannot get the wig on my head. My head is so sensitive. I had no idea. Also I had no idea how white my skin is. It is seriously white, dangerously white.

As shocking as it is to see my bald head it is not so much the absence of hair as the starkness of white skin that makes it so shocking. Back to the wig issue, I put the wig on last night and had a temper tantrum. I said I hated the wig. I called it Russian pussy hair. The hair on my wig is human. And it is from Russian hair. I do not know why I called it pussy hair. If it was pussy hair then it would not be a wig. It would

43

be a merkin. That is what a merkin is, a pussy wig. I had forgotten all that when I had my temper tantrum and screamed about my periwig and disparaged it by calling it pussy hair.

I get confused between merkins and gerkins because they are words that I rarely use. And I have actually never used the items themselves, unless my wig is a merkin and I really have bought pussy hair for my head. That is not the case. But I am having issues with my hairpiece. I should not. Some of the greatest present day Americans have been wig wearers. For example Tammy Wynette wore a wig. Dolly Parton wears wigs. I should be so lucky to be in their company for whatever the reason.

Maybe I should pretend that I have the wig for reasons other than chemotherapy caused balding. Maybe I should pretend that I am a barrister or a country singer, anything other than a cancer patient. Maybe I should be grateful that I don't have head lice and I was thus forced to shave my head for hygienic reason and I wear a wig because it is cleaner than head lice. Everything is attitude. I need to get a better attitude about my wig. But no matter what my attitude is it still does not alter the fact that I have issues with my wig.

I was an extra on the Dolly Parton Show about twenty years ago. It was really fun. I saw some of Dolly's wigs in the dressing room area. Those were some big hair wigs. Dolly Parton was really nice to me and my friends. She posed for a picture with us. Her hair looked better than my hair did. She was wearing a wig. I was wearing my hair. Her wig looked better than my hair. So what does that mean? Do I hate my wig because it is a bad wig or that my head is bad? Did Dolly's wig look great because anything that Dolly does is great? I think everything that Dolly does is great. I think that my wig is not that bad. I do not think my hair is bad. Well actually I think it is bad now because there is none. I looked at the photograph again and actually my hair looked pretty good, better than my wig looks. My wig is big hair.

Big hair used to be fairly popular. But it has never been popular on my head. And maybe it is no different for someone who is used to having big hair and then no longer has big hair. I suppose it is all what we are used to.

I was an extra on the Dolly Parton Show because Tammy Wynette was performing on the Dolly Parton show as one of the guests. Tammy had asked me if I wanted to come and hang out while they prepared for the show and then be an audience member/extra on the show. I brought two friends of mine who adored Dolly and Tammy, Sue and Peggy. We were each so excited. Every day we rode in the limo from our hotel with Tammy and her husband Richie onto the studio lot and into the studio. Tammy's hair was big. Tammy's big hair was a wig. I think that Tammy was used to seeing herself with big hair. It had to have been that way for years for Tammy because for years Tammy had big hair.

When I met Tammy Wynette she did not have big hair. In fact she had almost no hair at all. It was 1986, October of 1986. Tammy was standing in a cafeteria line at Betty Ford's. I had arrived a few days before on October 17, 1986. I had checked myself in because I was drinking too much and had been drinking too much for quite a while. Not that many people were aware of how much I drank because I was functional and proud. I did not want people to know how dependent I had become on alcohol. So I drank by myself so that no one would see me drunk. I had battled with binge drinking over the years. I never had a great deal of success. I was just lucky and never did anything totally outrageous or got caught for having done something terribly illegal.

I was 31. Tammy was about 13 years older than me. Tammy was at Betty Ford's because of addiction to pain pills. When I saw her she looked so small. She was wearing a turban to cover her very short hair. She wore the turban because she was used to wearing very big wigs and for whatever reason Tammy had decided not to bring her wigs to Betty Ford's. I walked up to her as she stood in the cafeteria line and said to her, "I am sorry that you have to be here and also so glad that you are here because I have always wanted to meet you." She smiled and asked my name. I told her. I helped her with her tray and we sat and chatted. And so that is how our friendship started. It was a friendship that lasted the rest of her lifetime until her death in 1998.

It is a friendship that made for more stories than Tammy had wigs, and she had a lot of wigs. Betty Ford's was expensive, but relatively speaking, for high-end treatment programs, Betty Ford's is the best deal in the United States. I had a lot of shame around my alcoholism. I liked drinking. I really did not want to stop. I just wanted to take a little vacation from drinking. I had been drinking heavily for awhile. I had tried bouts of abstinence with moderate success. But over time it had gotten harder and I did not feel much success about anything.

I had been a lawyer for 6 years. I had been a deputy district attorney for Ventura County and then San Mateo County for half of that time. Deputy District Attorneys are prosecutors. I joke about that time that I committed as many felonies as I prosecuted because at the time I did a fair amount of drugs. That really is not very funny. And it really is very true. And that really is very wrong. But there are a lot of wrong things within the criminal justice system. It really is not fair. But what in life is fair and who is to say what fair is. But thus far I have made a career saying what is not fair.

My head is so white and smooth and weird looking I can hardly think. But I will keep typing rather than get up and go and look at my head. Except the reader has no idea what I am doing. The reader cannot tell what I have done in between words or sentences. But I am telling the truth. I am typing and not looking and I think it is better that way.

I did not have the money to go to Betty Ford's. When Betty Ford's opened in 1983 I wanted to go there. I believed in Betty Ford and I believed in the Betty Ford Center. I am not sure why. I liked that the Betty Ford Center was in Rancho Mirage near Palm Springs. I love that area. I love the mountains. I love the heat. I love the strip. I love riding the tram to the top of the mountains and hiking around at 12,000 feet and being cold and then taking the tram back to the desert floor and being overwhelmed by the heat. I love how warm it is at night. I love how bright the stars are. So I was pleased when Betty Ford decided to open her treatment center in Rancho Mirage. When it opened I said to myself that is where I should go but I still was not ready.

I liked drinking. Drinking was my solution to any problem. Unfortunately in a relatively short period of time my solution was soon creating a whole new set of problems. For years I was problem solving by drinking and making new problems by things I had done when I was drinking. It was crazy really. But I did not know any better, nor was I really willing to act any differently. In many ways drinking worked. I would rather drink than process my feelings about being raped. I really had not developed feelings other than anger. Instead I drank. And it worked until it did not work anymore.

The end of my drinking is actually connected to cancer. In the early 1980s I had a girlfriend who was a police officer. I met her on a ride along when I was a deputy district attorney. We liked each other, but we were each seeing other people. I was still involved in an on again off again way with a Norwegian electrician who has since become a journalist for the Norwegian gay magazine called Blikk. Her name is Elin. The police officer and I would see each other every now and then, usually on jury trial days. I kept trying to get one of her cases to trial. I thought I would impress her with my prosecutorial skills. I would have if we ever got to trial but everyone she arrested just pled guilty. That probably says more about her selection of who to arrest than my trial skills. But that is not the point. The point is that we eventually got together. Soon after we began our relationship her mother's breast cancer came back. Only when it came back it had metastasized to her liver. That was the spring of 1984.

# 10

# JANE'S DEAL WITH GOD

The police officer, Cathy is one of the most striking women I have ever seen. It was true then and it is still true now some 22 years later. She is tall and blonde with blue eyes. Her face is attractive. Her body is strong. She is striking. Cathy looks like the female version of the David. Her muscles are chiseled and defined. Her shoulders are broad and strong, and her back is even broader and stronger. Cathy may have been given some genetic gifts, but Cathy became who she became because she put all of those gifts to work.

Cathy was a world class athlete. She had been world class since her early teens when she blossomed as a track and field athlete specializing in throwing the javelin. She was a great basketball player and a great volleyball player but her prowess throwing the javelin was world class. Throwing the javelin is an art. It requires strength, speed, and incredible skill. The motion is so unnatural because it is not at all like throwing a ball or any other implement. It is like throwing a toothpick. I have tried many times to throw a javelin far and I am a good athlete, but I just could never throw one that far. That far is defined as anything over 125 feet, and that is really good. Cathy threw the javelin over 200 feet in a meet in 1985. That was before she broke her ankle and never really recovered and eventually quit competing.

In 1984 Cathy's goal was to make the United States Olympic Team. She had been training for years to make an Olympic team. Cathy came in 4th place in 1976 at the age of 17 and just missed making the team. 1980 was the Olympic boycott. So 1984 was Cathy's year. Cathy had been working towards that goal since childhood. She had run and trained and lifted and thrown for most of her life.

I weight lifted with Cathy in the spring of 1984. Cathy is a great power lifter and she taught me a lot about lifting, enough so that I won a few lifting competitions. That was fun. I still have some of the trophies. But trophies were nothing new to me as I had won lots of trophies for swimming and tennis and softball. But Cathy's competition was at a new level, at the highest level, at the world class level. Cathy could Olympic lift as well as any man in the gym. Her technique was perfect and her dedication and discipline as good as her technique.

All was going pretty well in the spring of 1984 until March when Cathy and I were in Lake Tahoe for a vacation. We met her mother Jane who was there on vacation with her sister-in-law. Jane had gone to Tahoe for a vacation and to get away and to figure out how she was going to tell Cathy that her breast cancer had come back. I really did not understand what that must have meant to Jane or Cathy back then. I knew that it was bad. Cancer is bad. I just did not know what it meant to have cancer. At that time what I knew about cancer is that it would kill the person who had it and that it would happen fairly quickly.

Years before, my friends Ann and Mary, twins who I life guarded with, had a brother who got colon cancer. Almost as soon as they told me that their brother had cancer and that their parents had gone to California to be with him for his surgery, they then told me that he had died. My mother bought their airplane tickets for the funeral in California so they could join their parents and their deceased brother. He was young, only 27. So I knew that cancer was bad.

On that night that we had dinner together at some Italian restaurant in Lake Tahoe, Jane told me about the first time that she had cancer. The first time Jane had cancer was some twenty years earlier, when Cathy was just a little girl and her brother Bob was just a little boy. Cathy was about 6 or 7 and Bob was 7 or 8. Jane told us that she got the diagnosis. That was in early 1964, a really long time ago in medical years, a time so long ago that the doctors offered very little hope. Jane had a mastectomy. Jane let the doctors do all they could do. Jane also said that she bargained with God. She asked God to give her enough time to raise her children. There was a certain urgency to that request because Jane properly doubted her husband's ability to raise Cathy and Bob.

Jane's husband (and Cathy's father) always had a problem with drinking. Jane knew it shortly after they were married, but she had two small children and people stayed together then. I used to think the stress of living with her husband and worrying what he would or not do next gave Jane the cancer. I don't know if that is true anymore. I do not know if stress has anything to do with who gets cancer. I do not know anything about how or why I got cancer and whether the choices I have made and the things that stress me out and the fact that I worry about virtually everything is at all responsible for my cancer. Whether her husband caused it or not who knows but I am sure he did not help.

Jane explained over dinner that she had made that deal with God, and that God had kept his end of the bargain. God had given her the twenty years that the doctors said were impossible so that she could raise her children. She said she thought that she had gotten the best of the bargain. Cathy was very sad. I was a little confused. Jane looked great to me. I did not understand how the doctors could find a disease in a person who looked by all accounts healthy. Also I really did not understand how cancer was treated. And I was worried because I knew that the Olympic trials were less than three months away. I worried how this would affect Cathy's training.

Jane's illness did affect Cathy. It affected all of us. Jane started chemotherapy right away. She went to Kaiser Hospital in South San Francisco for her infusions. She would spend several hours there just like I spend at the infusion center. Jane lost her hair. Jane was nauseous for the days following the infusions. Cathy watched and worried. I worried not just about Jane, but about Cathy worrying about Jane. Overall I felt pretty helpless so I just encouraged Cathy to train. I also started to understand why Jane had been so fervent in her plea to God some twenty years earlier. Her husband would come home drunk. He was no help at all. I worried that Cathy would kill him. I sat with Jane and she told me stories about Cathy. It was nice.

I remember the one about a father-daughter basketball night at her middle school. Jane was healthy. Years had passed since the cancer scare. Cathy waited at home for her father to come home and take her to father–daughter night. He never showed up and so Jane had Cathy go with a neighbor family. The middle school festivities were in full swing. The gym was decorated. Fathers were there. Daughters were there. They were playing basketball and then in the roar of father-daughter fun Cathy's father staggered into the gym. He was shit faced drunk and immediately created a commotion. Cathy was mortified. Jane wanted to live to protect Cathy from things like that.

Yet even in life Jane could not protect Cathy from her father, nor herself from cancer.

I always hated that story. I loved that Jane told me. But I hated that he did that. I hated that after all these years her husband still did things like that and really did not seem to fathom the effect such drunken conduct has on other people. Because he did that kind of behavior so consistently throughout Cathy's childhood I believed that my concern that in all the stress that Cathy would kill him was reasonable. Cathy is too controlled to kill anyone. If he were my father I might have killed him. That is why I worried.

During Jane's chemo her husband came home drunk sometimes. But he left us alone and we left him alone. It was as if he did not exist. It was terrible. Throughout this terrible backdrop Cathy continued to train. The chemo treatments passed for Jane and we all looked forward to the Olympic trials.

Cathy and I drove to Los Angeles a few days before the trials. We stayed at a motel not far from the Los Angeles Coliseum. It was not very fancy, but neither of us had much money then, so it was the best we could do. Cathy trained. I worried. I worried what would happen if she did not make the team. I worried how disappointed she would be. I did not want Cathy to have any more bad feelings. I worried that I was powerless. I was powerless over her mother's cancer, over her mother's cancer treatment, and over how far Cathy's javelin would travel as well as how far other javelins would travel. I just worried a lot.

On the day of the qualifying round Cathy was relaxed. She only threw one time making the qualifying mark. It was a good throw, not a great one, but it did not need to be. It was perfect. She qualified for the finals.

The competition for the three who would make the team was the following day. We actually had a relaxing evening. But I think that we both were worried. On the day of the competition Cathy went to the Coliseum to prepare and I went to LAX airport to get Jane. I picked Jane up at the gate with a wheel chair. Jane was weak and nervous. Jane was determined to see Cathy throw. Cathy was determined to make the Olympic team. Jane wore a USA bandana. Jane had lost so much weight since the chemo began. Her face was sunken. She had an unquenchable thirst so I got her some ice to suck on as I wheeled her out of the airport to the car. The airport would not let me take the wheelchair. In retrospect, I should have just taken the wheelchair. But at the time I really did not understand just how weak Jane was.

I lifted Jane into Cathy's pick-up truck and I drove from LAX to the Coliseum. I was nervous. I worried. I worried how bad traffic would be. I worried how I was going to get Jane from the car into the Coliseum. I worried that we were going to miss the entire competition. Jane was very weak, but she was determined to see Cathy qualify for the Olympic team. It was on the drive to the Coliseum that Jane told me that she has bargained to stay alive to see Cathy compete in the Olympics. I still worried that the better bargain would have been to guarantee Cathy a spot on the Olympic team. But Jane was convinced. I worried. When we got to the Coliseum my heart was pounding with worry. Now I know what my mother's life must have been like when I was a kid. I do not think that my mother ever enjoyed watching me compete. I think she just worried. That is what I was doing. My heart was pounding so hard I thought I was going to throw up. I worried how I was going to get Jane from the car into the coliseum.

This was 1984. Cell phones did not exist so I did not have the option of calling for help. Instead I parked the car and carried Jane into the coliseum. I smoked then. After I carried Jane into the coliseum I went and had a cigarette. I did not leave Jane alone. Friends of

Cathy's were at the coliseum, who were there to support Cathy as well as compete in their own events. They stayed with Jane while I smoked a cigarette and worried.

There is a ritual to throwing a javelin. All throwers have their own rituals. They go out to the field. Most carry a big gym bag with the logo of their sponsor company. Cathy did not have a sponsor. One company gave her javelins. Another company gave her a few pair of shoes. No one gave her a bag. I think she carried a California Highway Patrol bag but that may not be true. The throwers set themselves down and put on their throwing shoes. They continue the warm-ups and stretches that they began well before entering the field.

All 12 of the finalists did just that. It is by lot that the order is determined. All 12 get three throws. After three throws then the top 8 throwers are allowed another three throws. The three persons who have the farthest throw at any round in the competition are the ones who would make the 1984 Olympic Team. Most of the other throwers did nothing but throw javelins and all the things that one does to get ready to throw javelins, like run and lift weights. Cathy did all that and also worked full time as a California Highway Patrol Officer.

Jane was nervous too. She had quit smoking years before the first time she was diagnosed with cancer. I did not enjoy my cigarette. I was too worried about Jane and her cancer, about Cathy and her throwing, and my own sense of inadequacy and the fact that I was at an athletic event, the US Olympic trials, and that I considered myself an athlete and there I was smoking.

Javelin competitions are time consuming. In the finals all throwers throw the first three throws. The first round took about an hour and a half. The next three rounds took almost an hour. I was worried and stressed and watched and cheered. Jane was profoundly confidant and really happy. I tried to hide how I felt about everything. At the end of the competition Cathy's fifth throw was the second longest. She was an Olympian. Jane smiled and cried. As thrilled as Jane was I was that relieved. Cathy joined us after the competition. Cathy was ecstatic. We celebrated and hugged.

Cathy took her mom to the airport to go home so that they could have some time together. I went back to the hotel. I was so wound up, not happy not sad, just worried. And nothing, not all of the beer or the cigarettes, seemed to calm me down. I always wanted to be on an Olympic team. I was not jealous of Cathy. I felt happy for her and proud of her. But I definitely felt as if I was not good enough. I made a vow that I would work harder and that I would be someone. If I would not be an Olympian then I would be someone.

The Olympics were awesome. I went to Opening Ceremonies and that made me cry. Not because they were so moving, which they were, but because I could not grasp how I ended up at the Olympics as a spectator and not as an Olympian. Cathy's mother's cancer went into remission just after the trials. So Jane was stronger at the Games. Cathy's father and Jane came to the Olympics. He was on his best behavior. We all sat together including Cathy's dear friend Leslie. We had a good time. I worried when Paul got a beer that he would get drunk and make a scene. But he did not.

The javelin qualifying rounds were at the same time as the end of the first Olympic Woman's Marathon. Joan Benoit Samuelson won the race. She came in strong. She was awesome. The stadium erupted. She crossed the finish line to the cheers of some 80,000 people. Joan Benoit Samuelson draped herself in an American flag and took a victory lap. Javelin throws punctuated the marathon finish. I only cared about two things: Cathy throwing the javelin far and me being somebody. Cathy had a good day and made the finals. I still worried about being someone.

The following night was the finals. The competition procedure was just like any competition except that this was the Olympics. Cathy did throw far and came in 10th- a drug free 10th. That was confirmed because Cathy was randomly tested. After the event we relaxed and celebrated with her friends and family at the hotel. That night Cathy stayed at the hotel rather than in the Olympic village. None of us could drive. We fell asleep with the television on. Somehow we woke up as the television station was signing off. This was in the days when television was not 24 hours a day-BC- before cable. The station was playing the National Anthem showing an American flag waving on the screen. We each woke up and looked at the television. I said, "The T.V. won the gold." And we laughed.

I think Cathy was pleased with her performance. I think Cathy was pleased that she made the team. I know her mother was ecstatic, so much so that her cancer went into remission. I think Cathy was more pleased about her mother's remission than she was about making an Olympic team. I was pleased that Cathy made the team and did well. I was pleased that Jane was happy and that her cancer was in remission. But I was not happy. I did not tell anyone. I just worried whether or not I would ever be somebody. And that is the joke, isn't it. I did not like myself enough to acknowledge that I am somebody. Instead of looking at the reasons why I felt so bad about myself I just worried about how I could be somebody.

# 11

# WHEN JANE DIED

Jane's cancer did not stay in remission. At the time of the Olympics, Jane's doctors were amazed by Jane. We all were. Jane had made one deal with God. It had seemed that God was keeping his end of the bargain. Jane had been alive for 19 years since her twenty year ago bargain with God. At that time only Jane knew about the bargain. Jane told us all in 1985 when the cancer returned with a vengeance. It was her twentieth year. Cathy was grown. Cathy was an Olympian, a college graduate, a sworn police officer, a woman any mother would be proud of. Jane was proud of Cathy. Bob was grown. He was doing well. She had raised both of her children. That was what she had asked from God, and what God had given to her. Jane had been given the time to raise her children.

The cancer came back to Jane before Jane had even realized it was back. The cancer came back to Jane before any of us realized the cancer was back. None of us understood what it meant for Jane that the cancer was back. She tried more chemotherapy. That did not work. The cancer had spread to her liver. Her liver grew and grew with cancer and Jane got sicker and sicker.

By October 1985 we all knew it was bad for Jane. One month later Jane started making arrangements for her death. She changed the deed to her house so that she could leave her half of the house to her children. I had never actually seen a person die before. I had been to lots of funerals in my life. I had never cried at a funeral because I had never really cried. I was emotionally short-circuited in those days.

Jane died at home in November 1985. Cathy, Bob, Leslie, her father and I were there. Jane had been in a coma. Jane had been in terrible pain for a few days. Cathy had given her morphine suppositories. But the pain won over the morphine until the cancer won and Jane's heart stopped and the cancer was as dead as the rest of her. Funny thing about cancer is that in trying to live it kills its host, very stupid on cancer's part. So cancer is anything but smart. Cancer is very stupid.

When I got my diagnosis I thought about Jane and all the people I knew who had died of one kind of cancer or another. I worried that the cancer had spread. I have seen what it does when it spreads. It is deadly. I gave the eulogy at Jane's funeral. It was a tear jerker. I wanted it to be that way. If I could not cry I wanted to say words that would cause others to cry. That is what happened. I drank a lot after that. I did not know what else to do. I drank heavily until I went to Betty Ford's. I have been scared since that time to get cancer. That is what has marked my perspective about my diagnosis.

# 12

# FEELING SORRY FOR MYSELF

I feel like shit today. I feel sorry for myself. I hate every one and everything. I am so angry. I am so confused. I made a mistake. I went on the internet. I looked up articles about chemotherapy and basically concluded after reading the many and varied articles that it is totally random who gets well. It is as random who eliminates cancer, or who gets cancer eliminated from them as it is who gets breast cancer to begin with. It is that random, it is just a smaller sample. That fact almost pisses me off more than the randomness of who gets cancer. These are doctors and chemists, people of science, and for all that they do, it appears to be random who dies and random who gets cancer back and random who continues to live with cancer.

So I go though all this chemofucking therapy with all these chemofucking drugs whose origin I barely understand, whose side effects I am as afraid of, almost as much as the cancer. Two days to go and then more poison. Lucky me. I am so angry, sad, scared and disassociated.

It is Sunday morning, June 9, 2007. It is the day before. My chemo day has been changed from Tuesday to Monday. So tomorrow is chemo day. Tomorrow at 1:30. I was crazy yesterday. I cried a lot and worried. I spent far too much time on the internet. I looked up breast cancer. I looked up Taxol and Herceptin and neoadjuvant, radiation, metastatic, and all these other words that really had no real meaning to me. Now they do not have much more real meaning because there is an opinion, a bias, a something as to all the words depending on who wrote them or when they were written or what they were written for. And in that context and with that knowledge I am trying to understand why it is that my oncologist has recommended the protocol that I am on.

I thought that I had basic breast cancer. I thought that I have a tumor in my left breast. I thought that luckily my cancer has not gone anywhere else. I thought that because I did a CAT scan, a PET scan, a bone scan, an MRI, and a liver ultra sound, all before I made a decision about my course of treatment so I could make the best decision possible on the theory that information contributes to good decision making, that I understood what I have. I am not so sure anymore.

Because I spent the day on the internet yesterday I am filled with doubt or fear or both. When I got the CAT scan I had to drink a banana flavored barium milk shake at 8 a.m. It was about 16 ounces of barium, which is 16 ounces of terrible. It took almost 15 minutes to choke it down. It tasted terrible. The only thing the banana flavoring did was make me hate bananas. The MRI day was a big day and it feels like it was years ago. But I did all of those tests so that I would have information and could make good decisions. And I wanted to know if there was cancer in places other than my left breast.

After I drank the banana barium milk shake I took a walk with Manaswar on the beach and burped up and down the bad banana barium milk shake. I showered. I am thinking back how great a shower that was because I still had my hair, which I got to wash, condition, comb, brush and look at. I got dressed in comfortable clothes for my day at the hospital.

I checked in at the Registration Desk at St. Luke's. The Registration Desk is really the billing center. They make sure that the patient has insurance to cover the cost of the treatment and that the insurance company will cover the cost of the procedure. I had been at the St. Luke's Registration Desk almost every day for a week at that point. The people there recognized me. I went there by myself. Woody did not come as we decided none of the procedures were any big deal.

It was at that point I first realized that what I was doing had been done by many, many people before me. I was so standard. I knew I was standard because my health insurance had willingly covered each and every procedure, without question. That is how I knew I was standard, because the whole process was standard. One in seven women get breast cancer. So for all the women that came before me who had to initially bicker or bargain to get authorizations from health insurance companies I give my thanks and offer my condolences because it sucks and I am sorry.

They checked me in at the Registration Desk. I went up to a waiting room for my CAT scan. I really did not know much about any of the procedures other than what I have seen on ER or Gray's Anatomy and those shows do not really show the tests as the tests really are boring to watch as well as to do. Steve the technician took me to a changing room and gave me a gown. I partially undressed. I covered my top in the gown and went to the CAT scan room with the star trek looking diagnostic machine, where Steve the technician and his trainee/ assistant were waiting for me.

I expected to be put on the gurney and slid into the plastic machine and get scanned. Instead when I got in the room Steve gave me another banana flavored barium milkshake and told me to drink it. This one took another 15 minutes to drink. Each gulp was punctuated by retching and gagging. I knew not to puke because it would invalidate the test protocol. I did not want to have to drink any more banana barium milk shakes.

After the shake drinking came the laying on the gurney. I just lay there. The gurney moved through the machine or the machine moved over the gurney. Whatever it was there was nothing to it on my part. It was really boring. I knew though that there was a second part to the test that included being injected with some radiation fluid that would make my body feel hot and the machine would take more pictures of my guts. I wondered what that would feel like. I had already decided that there was no other cancer in me so I pretty much felt that I was just doing all these tests to confirm what I believed and to gather information.

It did not take so long to do the first part of the CAT scan. Steve and the assistant/trainee retreated into another room when the machine was doing its testing. I think it must produce radiation or some such thing. I have always thought it was ironic that the testers need to be protected from the testing devices. But they are there all day. Hopefully for me this will basically be a one time deal.

After the first part Steve and the trainee emerged from the control room and readied me for part two of the procedure. Steve explained that they would connect me to an IV. I would experience a warming sensation from the materials injected into me. More pictures would be taken and then it would be over. Steve turned the insertion of the IV over to the trainee. The trainee was a nervous Pilipino man. I turned my head away. I hate needles. I hate blood. I especially hate needles that are being inserted into my veins and drawing my blood or having things put into my blood.

I turned to my right because the trainee was dealing with my left arm. I should have known I was in trouble when the trainee put the tourniquet on my left arm so lamely it felt more like an arm garter than a tourniquet. The tourniquet was a blue rubber band. It did nothing other than look blue. The trainee started poking. He poked and poked and poked. There was some pain, but certainly not unbearable. What was unbearable or rather became unbearable was the trainee's awkwardness and fear. I felt it. With each ambivalent poke I felt his fear. With each unsuccessful attempt to pierce my vein his fear grew and the next poke was even more ambivalently unsuccessful. After about the tenth failed poke I said "Enough" "You have got to do something different. You have got to do it on my other arm."

I turned my head to see their reactions. The trainee had tears in his eyes. He looked at me and said, "I don't like needles." I told him he had to be tough. He had to be butch. He had to believe in himself. He had to act with complete confidence. He had to believe he could do it. I said all that as I wondered why he had picked this as his profession. I am sure he had reasons. We always do.

The trainee appeared to collect himself. He did just as I instructed. The next thing I knew the IV was in my right arm. The fluid was coursing through my veins and the CAT scanned. They came back from the control room and I was done. The trainee gave me a big hug with tears in his eyes. He thanked me for the pep talk. The trainee I have heard is now this totally butch, awesome vein finder. Unfortunately for me I have now developed a phobia about having IVs inserted. Consequently I won't let any other trainees train on me.

After the CAT scan I went to the bone scan room and got my radiation shot in preparation for the scan about two hours later. That was easy enough. The bone scan tech was a friend of a friend of mine so that was fun. That made me comfortable. After the injection but before the scan itself I met my friend Lisa for coffee. We chatted and laughed. I went back to the hospital for the bone scan. That was more of the same. Just lay on a gurney while the tech retreats to the control room. I lay there. The machine moves or I move through the machine. Then it is over.

After the bone scan the tech, Carol and I talked. She told me what I already knew, that the scan looked clear. As it turns out Carol, the tech, had gone to India some almost thirty years ago with a good friend of mine. Carol told me all about their trip. They had gone to an ashram. I had heard my friend tell me of her great adventure years before. Now years later I heard Carol's experience. I have not been to the ashram in India yet. But one day I will go. I have gone to the ashram here in the bay area as well as the ashram in New York. I went to the ashram many times in the days before I began chemotherapy. I love that I have the ashram available to me.

In the time just after my diagnosis, our friends Suze Orman and her partner KT (Kathy Travis) were in San Francisco. Woody and I spent time with them, which was great, really great. For them to be in town when they are so rarely here felt extraordinarily lucky. I decided that their being in town was nothing less than grace. I am so lucky to have the people that I have in my life. I was determined to have that attitude in all my dealings with everyone in this whole process, which is really why I let the trainee do the IV the second time.

My conversation with Carol, the bone scan tech, was so good and fun I decided I was in such a good mood I would stop by and see Dr. Lora Burke, my breast surgeon. By now it was 4 p.m. I had not talked with Woody all day. Woody was recording. I did not want to interrupt her. Woody did not call me either. I walked into Lora's office. I spoke with her assistant Diana. Just as I was to ask if Dr. Burke was available Diana said to me words to the effect that it was so lucky for her that I had stopped by because she needed to make an appointment for me to have a liver ultrasound.

I freaked out. I knew what that meant. It meant that someone thought that there was cancer in my liver. I knew that if there was cancer in my liver that I was fucked. There is no polite diagnostic word for liver cancer. That is what happened to Cathy's mother Jane. Her breast cancer spread to her liver. Jane died of liver cancer. It was terrible. I made the appointment for early the following morning. I left without talking to Dr. Burke. I was no longer in a good mood. I did not want to talk to anyone.

I left the hospital and walked to my car. Just as I got to my car Woody drove past me in her car. She parked the car and then saw me. I wondered what the fuck she was doing there and why she had not called me. I got angry. I was already afraid. I thought she was going to be told something that someone should have told me especially because it is my liver. I confronted Woody "Why are you here?" She was happy to see me but I would have none of it. Eventually she calmed me down. We went together back to Dr. Burke's to find out what was really going on.

Dr. Burke was kind and precautionary about the necessity of a liver ultrasound. I was appropriate at her office. But when we got home I ranted and screamed and behaved badly. There was not a lot poor Woody could do. And that is what yesterday was like, that cross between fear and anger and sadness and self-pity. With tears and cursing while internet surfing intermittently punctuating what I made into a miserable day.

# 13

# WEARING A TURBAN
# ON TELEVISION

Those self-pity times happen. I have noticed they happen after times when I get really happy. I may be bipolar. But I like the extremes. I was happy the day before yesterday. I had been to court on Friday and my client who the prosecution wanted to send to prison ended up with only a county jail sentence. I wore a good suit and a nice scarf on my head. Everyone was incredibly nice. When I left the court house I checked my cell phone for messages and after the many messages there was message from Tamara at KRON4, a local television station. Of the many messages Tamara's call was the first I returned.

Tamara wanted to know if I would "come on set" to discuss the Paris Hilton case. Paris Hilton had been jailed for 45 days for violating her probation in an alcohol related reckless driving case. The Los

Angeles County Sheriff had the day before released her from jail and placed her on house arrest. This had caused the sentencing Judge to order her to appear back in court for a hearing regarding why she should not be put back in jail. The judge ultimately ruled that Paris Hilton should be put back in jail. Paris Hilton was led from the courtroom crying for her mother and yelling, "this is not fair."

Truer words had never been spoken by Paris Hilton. But nothing in life is fair. The criminal justice system is not fair. Hauling a wealthy heiress off to serve a sentence that in my 28 years of practicing law none of my similarly situated clients had ever received did seem manifestly unfair. Her heiress status actually worked against her. I am not sure that she was particularly well represented. There are a lot of nuances with alcohol related driving cases and mandatory license suspensions. But that is another story. The point of my story is that KRON wanted me to appear on the 5 o'clock and 6 o'clock news to discuss the case.

At first I said no I did not think I could do it. And then I said to Tamara, "I have breast cancer. I just lost all of my hair. I won't wear a wig, but I do wear a scarf and it looks pretty good. So if that is okay with you, I will do it." I cannot remember if Tamara put me on hold or not but she did tell me that of course that is great and they want me. So I agreed.

I did a TV piece about three weeks before. I still had hair then. That piece was for Channel 3, the NBC affiliate. It was not fun. I think the reporter wanted me to criticize someone for something that I did not believe warranted criticism. I won't do that. I won't say what people want me to say just to get to be on TV. So it was not fun at all. I had pretty much decided not to do any more TV things until after the chemo. But this sounded really fun. Also I thought Woody would have fun because we could go to the studio together and be there together and have a good laugh. It was not life or death. It was Paris Hilton.

When we got to KRON I introduced Woody to all of the news anchors. Woody and I sat on set for much of the broadcasts. We toured the newsroom and the studios. We had a really good time. It was a little stressful getting ready. I had been to the doctor's that afternoon and met with Angela the oncology nurse. Angela is great and Australian. I always feel good after I have seen her, which is why I should not go on the internet, because I never feel good after I have looked at stuff on the internet. I told Angela I would be on television that afternoon. I rushed home to change back into my court clothes and scarf.

Not having any hair saves a lot of time. Without hair I can shower, dress, and be ready in less than ten minutes. When I had hair it took three times that long to get ready. After dressing I realized I did not know where my makeup kit was. I do not normally wear makeup, but I do put a little on when I do television. Often times when I did cable news shows the show would provide a makeup person who would do me up. The manner of the make up artists varied. Each had their own conception of how I should look. Some I liked better than others. But it was always fun being pampered and given that special attention. But KRON was experiencing financial difficulties so there I did my own makeup. I could not find my makeup bag. I screamed at Woody to help find it. Woody looked in the cars. I tore threw my closet. Eventually Woody found the make up kit in the car. I applied a little and we were off to the studio.

We had a blast at the studio. I did my thing and did it well. We returned home happy and ready to go get a great dinner. When we walked in the door the dogs barked with glee. Their food source (us) had arrived as we had been at the studio at their regular dinner time. I noticed Manaswar because she is my dog. Manaswar is the mastiff.

69

Woody noticed Floyd because Floyd is her dog. Floyd is an 11 year old male brindle whippet. Floyd whines. He has always been a whiner. Floyd is high maintenance. But this night Floyd would bring new meaning to that term. I did not notice but Woody did. Floyd was sort of listing and leaning into the couch and a wall. Manaswar wanted her dinner. So Manaswar was my focus.

I fed Manaswar. Floyd did not want his dinner. That was not unusual as Floyd has always had unusual eating habits. Floyd eats in his own time and what he wants. Woody and I made an entry into the video diary. We got ready to go to dinner. I went into my bedroom and then into my bathroom. It was then that I realized that Floyd had gone into my closet while we were at the studio. Floyd had rummaged through my closet and found a bag of marijuana food products that a client had given me. Floyd picked a brownie to eat. The brownie was hidden, apparently not very well.

Floyd ate the whole marijuana brownie. I shouted to Woody about what Floyd had done. Woody now understood why Floyd was listing like a drunken sailor. We freaked. Floyd looked and acted more and more stoned. I called some doctors and most had no experience with a stoned dog. The common theme of all of the calls though was laughter. But I was freaking out. If anything happened to Floyd, Woody would be devastated. I would feel terrible because I should have hidden the brownie better.

I checked the internet about what to do and actually found an article in the Journal of Veterinary Medicine that was right on point. I read it and reread it. I did as the article directed. Floyd's highness developed to what I am sure was a full blown canine acid trip. We flipped him about every two hours. We monitored his breathing and his heart rate. I did not sleep much on Friday night because I had to worry and watch Floyd.

When morning came Floyd was still pretty stoned but definitely better. Woody had a gig with her friend Marca Cassity. They were playing at a festival in Santa Rosa at noon on Saturday. Woody was tired when she left for her gig. I was assigned to stay and take care of Floyd- to get him to walk and drink and wake up. As soon as Woody left I called to Floyd to come for a walk. Floyd did get up and staggered to the living room. He wanted to go for a walk. So we did. With each hour Floyd came closer to being himself to the point that by Saturday night Woody and I joked perhaps we should give him a little marijuana every night. That is a joke.

But it was in the time of taking care of Floyd and worrying about Floyd that I went on the internet and looked at all the sites with all the words that led me to the conclusion that who gets better from cancer is as random as who gets cancer. That scared me to tears. I do not know what is true. I do not know if I should even look at anything on the internet. But I do know that all of the pot that my many clients have given me to combat the chemo nausea is so hidden that Floyd will never get at it again.

# 14

# THE THIRD INFUSION

How bad can it get? It can get bad. It is bad. I went for my third chemo infusion on Monday. They gave me extra Ativan because at the last infusion I said I did not feel anything from the Ativan, which was a lie. But they believed me. I was making a joke when I said I felt nothing because I always feel something. No matter how much of what they give me it is never enough. So on Monday they gave me more than enough. I staggered out of the infusion center loaded out of mind.

When I got home there were friends waiting. I babbled and listed and acted remarkably like Floyd when he ate the pot brownie. I passed out. Woody probably turned me much like we did Floyd, but when I woke up on Tuesday morning I was nauseous beyond prior experience. I debated about whether to take the antinausea meds and decided against it. The anti nausea meds have their own set of side effects. The way they work I am still nauseous I just don't know that I am nauseous. That does not feel right to me. I would rather know what is really happening. So what is really happening is incredible nausea.

I try to drink water as much as I can but even drinking is a struggle. I sleep and my dreams are like acid trips. I did acid when I was in law school not a lot but enough to be able to say with some authority that my dreams now are like acid trips. That is not bad just very intense. I like intense.

I cannot sleep all of the time. I would if I could but I can't. So I write. I cannot talk too much because talking makes me nauseous. Even thinking about nausea makes me nauseous. It is weird. The power of the mind is incredible.

I have received a few phone calls from reporters, both print and television for quotes or to do interviews. I have declined. I tell the truth, that I have breast cancer and just did chemo and look like I am from Auschwitz or Darfur and just had chemotherapy. The point is I look like shit. I do not want to be broadcast over the airwaves looking this bad. I am vain.

Also I do not want to say the wrong thing. Though I hardly know what the right thing to say is. The topic of interest is not Paris Hilton. The topic of interest is the sentencing of a lawyer named Troy Ellerman. Troy Ellerman pled guilty to multiple counts of obstruction of justice and perjury in connection with showing grand jury transcripts to two San Francisco Chronicle reporters. The reporters then reported the contents of the testimony of Barry Bonds, Gary Sheffield, and Jason Giambi in the Chronicle. The baseball players had testified before a federal grand jury in San Francisco in the late fall of 2003. The leaked testimony was published in December of 2004.

December 2004 was a crazy time. The Scott Peterson trial was still the focus of everyone's attention. I was in Redwood City early that morning because I did an interview for CNN at about 5 am pacific coast time. I was too lazy and tired to drive back home before my next interview and before court started again. It was about 6 am. I went to get a cup of coffee. I looked at the newsstand and read the headlines "Bonds Denies Steroid Use". I knew from a quick glance that Gary Sheffield's testimony had been included in the article. I knew that with that article and the dissemination of that information that a whole new drama would unfold. I was right. It has unfolded, but at a snail's pace and with hypocrisy. The hypocrisy is greater than the slowness of the pace.

The case has come to be known as the BALCO case. The BALCO case is touted by many to be a very important case. But as with all information dissemination and opinions those who claim its importance do so to further their respective agendas. I represented Gary Sheffield when he appeared before the grand jury that issued the indictments against Victor Conte, Jim Valente, Greg Anderson, and Remy Korchevny. Barry Bonds testified before that grand jury as did Jason Giambi. Many other athletes testified before that grand jury. Most did not have their testimony leaked.

Troy Ellerman is the leaker. At the time that he did the leaking he represented one of the BALCO defendants, Jim Valente. Ellerman is being sentenced today in federal court for his role in leaking the transcripts as well as his actions in hiding the fact that he was the leaker. It is a big deal. What he did is a big deal. The effect of what he did is a big deal and continues to be a big deal. I sent a third year law student who is also my loyal and trusted law clerk, Justin Goodwin, to San Francisco Federal Court to watch the proceedings. I slept while Justin went to court. My dreams continue to be intense and acid-like. I think my dreams are like the dreams that the television character played by Patricia Arquette has in the show Medium. But mine are real. Yet they are dreams and not real.

I knew that Ellerman would not get sentenced that day. I knew that Judge White would not go along with the original sentence limitations contained in the plea agreement between Ellerman and the Government. I knew that before I sent Justin and before I went to sleep. So when Justin's call awakened me to tell me that Judge White had continued the case I was not surprised. I was mildly satisfied that my prediction was confirmed. The Balco story is an amazing story. I wonder if I have the energy to tell it. I wonder if I will live to tell it. I have a bias in my perspective. My bias is that I love Greg Anderson. Greg is currently imprisoned in the federal correctional facility in Dublin California. Greg is being held there as a recalcitrant witness. He has been in custody since November 2006, nearly seven months.

Under federal law a witness who refuses to testify before a grand jury after having been properly subpoenaed can be put in jail/prison for up to 18 months, or until the term of the grand jury expires, or until a court rules that the incarceration has become punitive and is no longer coercive. Greg was first subpoenaed in April 2006, about two months after he had been released from Atwater Federal Prison Camp where he had served three months as his punishment for his convictions in the original Balco case.

The original Balco case was overcharged and arguably misdirected. The subsequent Grand Jury proceedings border on ridiculous. Greg was subpoenaed by the very same federal prosecutors who relented in the plea negotiations in the original Balco case and no longer required Greg to "cooperate" as a condition of the plea agreement. What the Government originally wanted in terms of Greg's cooperation was that he "name names". Greg said he would not do that-ever. Greg said that from the very inception of the original Balco case. For some three years Greg had said through his lawyers that he would not name names. The Prosecutors, Assistant United States Attorneys, relented and dropped the cooperation requirement from the plea bargain with Greg. Greg pled to a few felonies, conspiracy to distribute steroids and a money laundering count. The crimes sound far more terrible than the actual conduct that gave rise to the charges. But that is how the criminal justice system operates. It is all spin. In this case it is not so much what Greg did or did not do, but rather who he did it with. There is no question that if the case did not involve Barry Bonds among others the case would never have ever been filed in federal court.

In October 2005 Greg was sentenced because of his guilty pleas entered in July 2005. Greg was sentenced to serve three months in prison followed by three months of house arrest. He got out of prison at the end of February 2006. Greg was served with the subpoena ordering him to appear to testify in what is known as the Bonds Grand Jury two months later. By that subpoena the Government sought to compel Greg to testify- essentially make him do what he said he would not do when they were going through the plea negotiations. They had offered him no jail in exchange for cooperation. Greg would not cooperate. He entered into a plea deal that he believed closed his involvement in all matters related to Balco, Barry Bonds, and any other person. Greg served his time at Atwater Penitentiary. I visited him there. That was before my cancer diagnosis. He did not see a grand jury subpoena coming. I am not sure that his lawyers did either. I actually believed that the Government had decided to leave him alone with the plea and sentence in the Balco matter. I was wrong.

When the prosecutors subpoenaed Greg I was shocked. So was he. When Greg would not "cooperate" he was imprisoned. Greg has served a total of 11 months in several different prison stints in the Government's efforts to compel him to testify. The Government can do all that because a federal trial court has ruled that the Government can do that. Then the Ninth Circuit Court of Appeals ruled that the trial court's ruling was proper.

So Greg sits in a shithole prison in Dublin California. It was after Greg had been there almost six months that I got diagnosed with cancer. Stress causes cancer. The stress of watching year after year the insanity of the criminal justice system may just have been too much for me. Watching the Government use its vast and powerful resources to imprison a very minor player who is just trying to escape any notoriety makes me grateful I am too sick to do anything. So Greg sits in prison and I have cancer. I sit at home nauseous and our miserable parallel existences pass a day at a time. I have not seen Greg for two weeks.

Before my diagnosis I saw Greg at least once a week in prison. Before Greg was imprisoned, which was before my diagnosis, I trained with Greg every day, except Sundays. Before my diagnosis but after Greg's imprisonment I saw Greg on Thanksgiving and Christmas and New Year's Day. I drove to the prison early on the holidays, before it gets crowded. It takes about an hour to drive out to Dublin, sometimes longer depending on traffic. It is a whole other world out there in Dublin. There are suburbs and large shopping malls and office complexes and lots of traffic. Most of the complexes are new, within the last ten years.

Santa Rita, the Alameda County Jail is in Dublin. The Dublin Federal Correctional Facility is located next door to the Alameda County Jail. The facilities were built before the housing complexes. When the prisons were built there was nothing out there. Now there is a lot out there and the jails look strangely out of place. The Federal facility is really two separate prisons, like some sort of Wrigley chewing gum concoction-two, two, two prisons in one. One prison is a women's prison and the other is a holding facility for men. Greg is in the men's prison-obviously. The prisons were built on an army base. The first time Greg was incarcerated for not "talking" was in June 2006. I went out to the prison and saw him the day after he was taken into

PAULA CANNY

custody in the courtroom and then taken to Dublin prison. Then I had to enter through the gate at the military base. I had to show my identification, driver's license and bar card before they would let me in.

I went out there every few days during that first round of incarceration. It was oddly invigorating. Greg was resolute. I was resolute. Mark Geragos, who had become Greg's lawyer, was resolute. I had done a great deal of research. I thought that we had very compelling arguments on Greg's behalf. I also knew that the grand jury before which Greg had just been brought was scheduled to end in mid July. This meant that when the grand jury's term expired Greg would have to be released. It meant Greg would only be kept in prison there for a few weeks. We both knew this. Our visits were intense and hopeful. My favorite trip to Dublin was the day that Greg was released because the grand jury's term had expired.

The prison had called me and told me that I could pick up Greg at 1:00 p.m. The army gate entrance was still in effect. I went through the army gate entrance. There were television crews at the gate. There were other television crews across the street from the actual prison. Everyone wanted a picture of Greg. I parked my car. I went into the prison. When I got in the door most of the prison administrators were there waiting for me. Some of the private security guards were there as well.

The Army base and Federal prisons were protected by a private security company, something like Atlas Patrol or some such ridiculous name. It always struck me as absurd that an army base and a prison did not have sufficient personnel to provide its own security. One time I asked one of the security guards why the army did not provide soldiers or the prison provide guards. He explained that army personnel had either been deployed to Iraq or were reservists and that the prison guards were not trained in premises

78

security. Maybe we should just send private security guards to Iraq. Oh, we have. Now I know why.

The private security guards told me that I would have to follow them to another gate, not the main gate to exit. They said they would unlock the gate allowing Greg and I to exit. I asked the administrators where Greg was- that he was due out by now. They assured me Greg was being brought out. Soon Greg came out. He was in his prison clothes, big baggie pale blue shirt and pants. He had a piece of paper in his hand. I knew what it was without Greg telling me. The delay was occasioned by the late arrival of federal agents who had been ordered to serve Greg with a new subpoena.

The piece of paper was a new subpoena. We both knew then that this would go on for much longer. I am not sure that Greg thought he would end up being put in prison for some 11 months and counting. I am not sure what I thought. But I did not believe then that the system would operate as stupidly as it has this far. But who says life is fair or that people are not stupid. It is random. I hope my doctors are smarter than lawyers, including me. And I hope that I am lucky.

# 15

# WORRYING ABOUT GREG

Greg sits in prison and I have cancer and both experiences are going to alter forever how we view the world and our place in it. Mine has been altered just watching Greg's experience. I think the same is true for Greg.

Today is Father's day. It is nine months since Greg has seen his son Cole. He has missed Cole's First Communion, his entire basketball season, his little league baseball season, Thanksgiving, Christmas, New Years, Cole's birthday, Greg's birthday, and all the other things that go with a father's love of a son. So what type of system would countenance incarcerating another person for not cooperating when the Government agreed to drop the cooperation from the original criminal case? The American system allows just what has happened. Sometimes principles take a back seat to egos. We are human after all.

The Assistant United States Attorneys handling the Balco case are white Catholic preppies in their late thirties and early forties. The United States Attorney who headed the San Francisco Office, Kevin Ryan, when Balco began is Catholic. He arranged the orchestration of the Balco fiasco. Kevin Ryan set up the boggled strategy for the prosecution. I believe Jeff Novitsky the Internal Revenue Service Agent who initiated the entire Balco case is also a Catholic preppie.

There is nothing like the self-righteousness of a Catholic educated preppie. Oops, I am a Catholic educated preppie. Really there is nothing like it. They are on a mission. Maybe I am on a mission and am no different from them. The law is their sword. Maybe the law is my shield. Moral authority and moral necessity guide them. Moral authority and moral necessity and cancer guide me. The ends justify the means. They do not always say that, but that is how it appears. There is collateral damage and it is rarely a prosecutor or anyone in law enforcement. I am afraid the collateral damage is me, is my cancer.

Greg is also collateral damage. I believe that the Prosecutors truly believe that it is Greg's fault that he sits in prison. They cannot fathom how he would not yield to their demands. If Greg does what they want him to do he could be free. They truly do not care that Greg said from the very start and truly it is the only thing he has ever said which is he would say nothing. They did not believe him. Their failure to believe him says more about them than it does Greg.

Sometimes Prosecutors prosecute with the moral superiority that comes from whatever source. Prosecutors develop a special sense of entitlement that only the powerful know. No Catholic woman ever has such an experience as a Catholic man. It is something only a Catholic man can have. Women are second-class citizens in Catholicism. I went to the oldest Catholic girls school in the

United States called Georgetown Visitation College Preparatory School for Young Ladies. It was founded in 1789. I attended private Catholic girls schools, once we got back from England. I know Catholic girls and I know Catholic boys. The Assistant United States Attorneys handling the case are altar boys with law degrees. I am still complaining that the altar boys can do something that I cannot do. I cannot get Greg out of prison under his terms. Greg could get himself out of prison under their terms. Therein lies the problem. It is a giant ego clash. They might say it is based on principles. Most ego battles are waged under the guise of principles. "For the principle of the matter" sounds so much more principled than "for the ego". And so it goes.

Most of the altar boys I know were the chosen ones. They truly were chosen. The priest chose them to be the one to wear the robes and hold the communion trays. I clearly still suffer from altar boy envy. After church the altar boys did what they wanted. They were held to a different set of rules. This is the Balco case. The U.S. Attorney did what he wanted and holds himself to a different set of rules than anyone else. The Catholic Church condemns the death penalty and yet Catholic United States Attorneys as well as Catholic Deputy District Attorneys prosecute death penalty cases. They betray their religious beliefs for the law. It must fuck with their heads at least a little. Yet they soldier on. And Greg is in prison and I have cancer and nothing feels very fair.

I have a history with one of the prosecutors. He was deputy district attorney for San Mateo County in the mid 1990s. He was and still is a great looking guy. I jokingly called him "Father" because he was so Catholically clean cut. He admitted to having been an altar boy. But I knew it from the moment I met him that he had been an altar boy. Our relationship was cordial enough. We each liked to work out and compete in athletic events. We kept things low key. Then I took a sex case that he was prosecuting. I do not do sex cases much any more mainly because I feel like I have done my time doing sex cases. That was the last time I took a sex case. I did not ever like doing them. They triggered my own experiences and my own traumas. The funny part was that I used to do them just to prove to myself that I was not affected by my own experience. Then I went to therapy, a lot of therapy, and learned that no matter what I say about not being bothered I was bothered. So I stopped doing sex cases.

"Father" was prosecuting my client, Mr. X. Mr. X has been through enough without being named by name here. X was charged with assault to commit rape and unlawful touching of a minor, both felonies. Conviction of either requires lifetime registration as a sex offender. I tried to work out a plea bargain that did not require registration. "Father" would have none of that. He wanted X to have to register. There were problems with the prosecution's case, which should have inured to a plea bargain resolution.

One problem was that the minor victim did not want to testify. Another problem was that her family was oddly indifferent to her turmoil as X is her uncle by marriage. There was family drama and dysfunction. The police also destroyed a videotape interview. I do believe that they destroyed it accidentally. The Judge let them testify as to their recollection of the videotape. Needless to say I objected on tons of grounds from Constitutional to statutory to practical and lost on all of them.

The prosecutor insisted that the minor testify. She did. She was uncomfortable and embarrassed and received little or no family support. I was fair in my cross examination of her. That she was damaged was apparent. The jury also found my client to be damaged and he was convicted. The 15 year old girl witness was abandoned by everyone who should have supported her including the prosecution. X was sentenced to jail. Two weeks later the minor committed suicide by hanging herself. The Prosecutor soon quit the San Mateo District Attorney's Office.

I felt terrible about her. I also felt sorry for the Prosecutor as I was sure that he had to have some guilt about his insistence that she testify, in spite of her reluctance, all to get a conviction that required the defendant to register as a sex offender. What a ridiculous trade off. I imagined that the deputy D.A. felt remorse that he had not understood the girl's dilemma. I had tried to explain it to him. Again and again I had tried to explain her dilemma. In pursuing the complaint the girl's mother put into action a course of conduct that the girl had never wanted. The girl had not wanted to make the complaint. But she told her mother that X had come into her room late the night before and tried to hit on her and even hugged and kissed her and that she had screamed at him to leave, which he did. Her mother made her get into the car and go to the police station to report the matter. The minor was compliant and did as she was told. That complaint set into action the writing of a police report, an arrest warrant, an arrest, and a prosecution. The girl had no idea any of that would happen. Since the making of the report, somehow the minor's mother and X reconciled in some way such that the mother no longer supported her daughter or the complaint. In fact the mother was now insistent that her daughter change her story. The truth is the girl was telling the truth. I tried to explain to the deputy D.A. that the minor had no support, that the family now sided with X.

The prosecutor would have no part of any of the collateral matters. There was a police report. There was a crime. He believed it was duty to prosecute to get a conviction. The minor girl was a means to that end. He got the conviction. The girl killed herself. I thought he felt bad or at least I imagined he did. Because I did. I felt badly. The girl needed support more than the criminal justice system needed a conviction. I just assumed that is how he felt after she killed herself. I just assumed he felt some measure of responsibility for her demise.

The prosecutor quit prosecuting for awhile. He went to work for a large civil firm in San Francisco. I went to a treatment program for depression. Although I had been sober since 1986 and regularly attended AA meetings, that girl's death was my final straw. I had a few issues in my personal life as well. I had worked and worked and done all these different things to not deal with my feelings. I worked on my issues and came to recognize all that bothered me. That girl's suicide was the straw that broke my emotional back. I decided that I had to deal with all that bothered me emotionally or I would end up just like that poor girl. I went to a place called the Meadows.

At the Meadows I learned to have a feeling at or near the time of the event that gives rise to the event that is appropriate to the event. In other words when something made me sad I could cry. I learned a lot there. I went there because I did not want to hang myself. I wanted to live and not feel despair. Now some 9 years later I am again trying to live. Gratefully I do not have any despair. I hate all of the cancer stuff and the treatment but I am happy. But that is not the point. The point is I had not thought about that prosecutor other than in passing for years and then I see him in United States District Court in San Francisco representing the United States of America as an Assistant United States Attorney. He was trying to compel Greg Anderson to testify in a grand jury proceeding or alternatively to incarcerate Greg until he would testify.

The moment I saw him in Court I realized I might have been wrong about everything about the girl who hanged herself and the Prosecutor. He may never have felt any of that which I imagined he had. Because if he had he would not be doing to Greg that which he had done to the girl who hanged herself. I knew Greg was in trouble when I saw the new Assistant U.S. Attorney. Prosecutors sometimes lose sight of what they are doing and how they view people, using their witnesses as a means to an end without giving much thought to the witness themselves. So Greg sits in jail and the former San Mateo Prosecutor waits as do the other assistant U.S. Attorneys. Barry Bonds just keeps hitting home runs. Each time Barry hits a home run I take pleasure in knowing that the law enforcement officers are filled with resentment and unable to celebrate the joy of a Bonds home run.

# 16

# NO MORE A/C

July 1, 2007

It has been a long time since I have written. I finished my fourth and last adriamyacin/cytoxin chemotherapy protocol. That was terrible. To allow someone to stick a needle in my arm attached to some tubes and then let them pump poison in my veins is crazy. It takes about four hours. Even writing about it makes me sick. Seriously I can feel myself, my mind absolutely fill with revulsion. Then there is some smell that my brain remembers and all of it together makes me sick-which means it makes me puke. So I will go puke.

This has been the worst few weeks. I really do not think I have ever done anything worse. I am bald. We shaved the stubble. So I am just cone head bald. My pubic hair is also going. That is weird. That area has been covered for some 40 years. Now that is a long time. I actually like pubic hair. I think it hides a multitude of old saggy skin. I suppose I would rather be hairy than saggy. But I am going to be hairless and saggy. 52 years of gravity pulling my twat down. A wig that covers lost pubic hair is called a merkin. Maybe I can restyle my wig and use that as my merkin. Except the wig, maybe merkin, stinks. I have a weird sense of smell. I smell some things vividly and other things that have odor I do not smell. It kind of does not make sense about what I cannot smell. I could not smell a skunk. The dogs and Woody all smelled the skunk but even when I tried I could not smell it. On the other hand Woody ate a cracker. I could smell the cracker on her breath from across the room. The smell of a wheat cracker made me nauseous. I cannot explain it. I do not really care what I smell. I only care about not puking or puking.

# 17

# ANTICIPATORY NAUSEA

I had Herceptin by itself this afternoon. I still freaked out. Actually my head freaked out. I laid on the gurney and cried and felt nausea, the opposite of euphoric recall. I still am having that nausea. It has been three hours since the infusion and I am still nauseous. I have not written in a long time. I have felt sick and sorry for myself. Woody and Joan just left to go for a walk. I made them kiss me goodbye. I told them that I still felt nauseous and that I am still worried about throwing up, and still felt like throwing up. I had hot dogs for lunch. I love all dogs, my dog dog and hot dogs. Joan suggested I just throw up. I said I hate throwing up wieners. I continued it is like a reverse blow job. Woody and Joan said that I am disgusting. They left me to take a walk.

I walked this morning on the beach with Manaswar, my dog, my mastiff. Now I am lying in bed and typing. My fingers are taking a walk. I have had some time to think over the past few days. I have not been so sick. I may have been wrong about Drug Court. All these years I have been telling people not to smoke pot, that drugs are bad etc. Well the only thing that has brought me any pleasure at all has been occasionally smoking pot. So maybe the way Drug Court should operate is that everyone has to smoke some pot before court even starts. Court would certainly be more relaxed. Maybe I have just been too uptight. Maybe I should just smoke pot and not worry. When I smoke pot I really do not care whether Annie Liebowitz or anyone takes my picture or whether I meet Vanessa Redgrave. Each would be an interesting experience but when I am high I just really do not care one way or another.

Cancer is terrible. Cancer is miserable. I hate cancer. I hate cancer. I had to say it again. My head is so twisted. I hate the chemotherapy when I ought to be hating the cancer. I have to adjust my attitude. Chemotherapy is what is going to save me. So it is so twisted of me to hate the chemotherapy and not address my feelings about the cancer. I do hate the chemo. I believe that I hate the cancer too, except there is some sick part of me that still hardly believes that I have cancer. I never thought that I would get cancer. I suppose the way I am dealing with this is distracting myself from the cancer by hating the cure. It is weird. As long as you are healthy enough to be treated the cure will always be worse than the cancer. But I am sure that for as terrible as the chemo is, and it is terrible, cancer is worse. First it does not start out so bad. It is just a little cancer. But cancer begets cancer and then cancer becomes this pacman attacker of everything until there are no healthy cells. That does not sound very nice. It kind of sounds like chemotherapy.

I have cancer. I have cancer. I have cancer. I should write the sentence over and over and maybe then I will believe it. I do not really think that I have cancer. I think that there is an intruder in my left breast but that I do not have cancer any other place. But whether I have cancer in one place or another place the point is that I have cancer. I am being treated with chemotherapy. I should love the chemo and hate the cancer. I have to remember that. The chemo is going to save me. The cancer would kill me. The goal of the chemo is to kill the cancer before the cancer kills me. So I am going to stop hating the chemotherapy and start loving it and start hating the cancer while saying goodbye to it.

In an effort to better convey all of the forgoing I think I should write a play. I have entitled the piece "Cancer-The Musical". It will be a musical and it will be funny. It will be informative and clever and it will be my creation.

Here goes: Cancer-The Musical…Opening song…middle age woman with very young energy…She begins singing…"I've got cancer…I do chemo…I've got cancer who could ask for anything more…" The song is sung to the tune I've got rhythm, I've got music, I've got… blahblah…"who could ask for anything more.." that is the refrain for the 'I've got cancer' song. The song needs more verses.

The only other song that I have thought of…oops now I forgot it… can I remember it…chim chiminy chim chiminy chim chim sharoo they poke me and stick me and they'll do that to you ….okay that was the song….I will have to listen to them all and get it all down… but this will be fun…I may have to open another document for my musical…but I have to get clear that chemo may be terrible, is terrible but hopefully the chemo kills the cancer before the cancer kills me. So go chemo. Maybe that should be in the musical….go chemo…go chemo…go chemo, like what we used to sing to Jody when we were on a princess trek in the Himalayas, only then we sang, "Go Jody, Go Jody." The song worked with Jody. She kept walking. I want the chemo to keep working.

I do not want to talk to anyone or do anything right now. I wish I could clear my head. I have to get my head right about getting IVs. I have to welcome the drugs into me and ask them to kick cancer's ass. So come on in chemo and kick cancer's ass. The rest of me can survive. So come on in Herceptin and kick some her2 ass.

That is enough for now. Maybe if I sleep my head will not be so crazy and nauseous. I really hate lying on the gurney bed. I covered my head with my sweatshirt. I have had far worse aches and pains than this and yet this is miserable. It is my head. The dogs are on my bed and the fear is in my head...hi ho the Dario...Should be...the fear is in my head...the dogs are on my bed hi ho the Dario the fear is in my head...enough for now.

# 18

# WALKING WITH MARTA

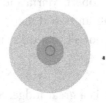

Saturdays even in the chemo week is my favorite day of the week. No matter how badly I feel I make myself get up early on Saturdays. I get up early to walk with Marta. At 7:30 a.m. I pick up Marta at her house. We drive a short distance to the causeway. We park the car. We walk around Foster City. We don't just walk. We walk and we talk. When we walk I wear a bandana on my head to hide my bald head. Marta never has cared about my bald head. She just walks with me. I walk with her and we talk. It is the most normal I ever feel. I feel strong when I walk with Marta. I feel loved and accepted. Maybe because I feel loved and accepted I feel strong.

We talk about everything when we walk. We talk about our mothers. Our mothers are remarkably similar. Our mothers are flaming liberals. Marta's mother grew up in an upper middle class family in Mexico City and still has a thick Mexican accent. She sounds elegant when she speaks. My mother grew up in Alameda California, the eighth of nine children in a poor family because her father had died when she was very young. My mother carried the American flag leading the ceremony procession when the Park Street Bridge, which connects the island of Alameda to Oakland, opened in 1928. She was 7 years old. Marta's mother, like my mother, went to Catholic schools. They were both beautiful and smart.

Our mothers did their own things. They were independent before it was fashionable to be independent. Our mothers did their best to raise us. They each married men named Robert and each gave birth to a second child, boys named Robert. Marta and I thus each have a younger brother named Robert. Marta and I are the responsible ones. When we walk we talk about how difficult it is to be the responsible ones knowing that it is not all that difficult and that we would not have it any other way.

Marta is a judge. Marta is a great judge. She is responsible for the funding and the building of an incredible juvenile court complex in San Mateo County. As great as the physical structure is the programs that she has started there are more incredible.

Marta is devoted and compassionate in her work and to everything she does. She is especially devoted to our Saturday morning walk and talks. I love that time. I enjoy walking and feeling for that hour or so that when we walk that I am not sick.

I have another friend who is also a Judge. But this friend is undergoing a breast cancer diagnosis and treatment. We got our respective diagnosis days apart. Our treatment has been somewhat different. Rose had a lumpectomy first and then did chemo. She is doing chemo now and then will do radiation. Rose is not working. She walks, when she can. We do not walk together as I am not sure that we have had two good days at the same time.

Marta and I have talked about all of the people that we know who have been diagnosed with various forms of cancer. As long as we are walking somehow it does not feel so bad. But when I stop to think about Rose or any of the other people I know who are going through what is a very terrible and difficult and stressful experience I just get sad. I really cannot even think about how terrible it is for anyone else because then I would have to acknowledge that this is terrible for me. It is easier just to walk.

After Marta and I walk we go to Noah's Bagels. The first time we walked after I started chemo we went to Noah's. I ordered what I usually order, a bagel with lox and cream cheese, capers, onions and tomato. That morning when I ate my usual I realized that the usual made me sick. I could not taste the usual. I never really told Marta that I could not taste my usual bagel. I acted as if I could taste it and that the usual tasted good. All summer I could not taste a bagel. But every Saturday I walked and went to Noah's and ate a bagel as if I did not have cancer, as if I was not sick from chemotherapy.

I feel safe walking with Marta. I feel self conscious about my bald head, even though it is covered so no one necessarily knows that I am bald. I feel self conscious about my pale, gray skin. I am self conscious that people see me and know that I am undergoing chemo therapy and that they see me as weak. I do not care what people think of me when I am with Marta because I believe that if anyone tried to hurt me Marta would get them. I like to feel normal, as normal as I ever feel.

During our walk Marta and I plan what movie we will take our mothers to see either Saturday afternoon or Sunday afternoon, and when and where we will go. Marta and I and our mothers have seen movies all summer long since I was diagnosed with breast cancer. My hair was long, and blonde when we started. Then I cut it shorter, and that cut got rave reviews. Then my hair started falling out and I got the GI Jane cut. When my hair fell out I started with the Pirates of the Caribbean look. That is the look that I wear to the movies. I know it looks like I am covering my bald head. But that is precisely what I am doing. Marta and the mothers tell me I look great. I know that is not true. But I like that they pretend. That makes it easier for me to just go to the movies.

# 19

# TOO SICK TO WRITE

August 7, 2007

Three weeks since I have written. It is now August 7, 2007. I have been too sick to write. I was so sick that Chombi my dear Sherpa friend came to visit from Nepal. He stayed for almost three weeks. He helped take care of me. I do not know where the three weeks went. A day at a time the days went by. The days were long and slow and sick, like a slog. Every part of me hurt. Some parts hurt more than others. The only interesting part of the experience is which body part would hurt more at any given time. I never knew what part would hurt when and where the body pain would manifest. Sometimes it was nausea. Sometimes it was diarrhea. Sometimes it was a headache. Sometimes it was vomiting. Sometimes it was joint ache. Sometimes it was random shooting pains in body parts that I never really knew to have pain, like the back of my eyeball or my cervix. I never knew what was coming and when it would come. This time was hard on Woody and Chombi because I was clearly in a lot of pain and not much helped.

I would not take pain pills as they have side effects. Occasionally I would smoke some pot and I could go to sleep. But most of the time I was in some weird dreamlike pain state that was like its own drug. And somehow three weeks passed. The three weeks passed with Greg in prison and various media outlets contacting me about interviews with Greg. The three weeks passed as Barry Bonds hit a home run here and there with the media hoopla growing to a bored crescendo waiting for him to break Hank Aaron's all time home run record.

Tonight Barry Bonds hit a home run in his third at bat with a full count after two hits, a double and a single. It was the 756th home run of his career and one more than Hank Aaron's career total of 755. Woody and I were videoconferencing with Suze and KT on our apples. They were in Florida and tan and almost sleeping. We were in Daly City. Woody has hair. I am still bald and white headed. Sure enough as soon as I did not care about what Barry did he went and hit the home run.

Today is an auspicious day anyway. Today is one year since Kailas died. It has not been a good year. Manaswar is limping. She hurt her back right leg and she is limping. I am worrying about her leg. I have not written because I cannot bear to even talk about it any more. Talk about joint pain and rogue pain. Parts of me hurt that I have never really known to feel anything. My cervix hurt. My asshole hurt. My stomach regurgitates some weird mucous that goes up and down my throat. I worry that I am dying. I worry that this will not work. I worry that I am not dying and that this has worked and that I will have to put in action all the resolves and bargains that I have made with God. Meanwhile, I just try to take it a day at a time.

It is hard to type tonight because they put the needle or shunt or the thing they stick in my veins to infuse the chemotherapy drugs in to my right wrist. Somehow something was not right and my right wrist has swollen. Yesterday my veins started cramping. I screamed. Who knew veins could cramp. They did. I didn't. They gave me some Ativan. But I want to type because I want to say how funny and not funny this all is.

Barry Bonds' head is as bald as mine. Barry Bonds' head is as black as mine is white. Who would have thought that my head and his head would be so intimately connected? At the post game press conference Barry was asked about Greg Anderson. Barry said that was bringing up a negative or some such thing and did not answer. I suppose what could he say. But I thought he could do better than that.

Greg is in prison in Dublin California at the Dublin Federal Correctional Facility. Greg is being held as a civil contemnor because he refuses to answer questions posed by some Assistant United States Attorney that they do not need to ask Greg. Prosecutors always want what they cannot have. Don't we all. But I do not want to talk about them. I want to talk about human relativity.

Barry Bonds earns 18 million dollars a year. 18 million dollars for one year of playing baseball. That is a lot of money. That is more money than most people earn in a lifetime. Barry Bonds earns that in one year for dressing in a uniform wearing the number 25 running around a field of grass on defense and ignoring or missing or hitting a ball and then running around a dirt field diamond on offense. It is a hard life in some ways. There are 162 games to play in a season, not including preseason or post season. It is a grind. Bonds also trains in the off-season. Half the games are played on the road. It is a hard life unless one loves baseball and then it is the greatest life. I think for Barry Bonds it has been the greatest life.

Back to just how much money 18 million dollars is. A person would have to work 36 years earning $500,000.00 per year to earn 18 million dollars. A half of a million dollars a year is a lot of money. Most surgeons do not earn half a million dollars a year. Barry Bonds earns that in a few weeks. No wonder there is some resentment towards Barry. Barry earns $100,000.00 per game. That is a lot of money. Barry Bonds earns $11,111.11 an inning. That is a lot of money. I wish I earned that for each chemo treatment.

Meanwhile Greg sits in prison. The prosecutors want Greg to talk. And Barry won't talk about a negative. I have no hair. My right wrist is swollen. I feel like I am going to puke. This is my life and we all have some connection to that homerun. Some will say that they were at the stadium. More and more as year after year passes will claim to have been at the game. I will always remember Barry Bonds broke Hank Aarons home run record in the summer that I had cancer, the summer that I had chemotherapy. The summer I could call my bald summer. That my head is as bald as Barry's head and Greg's hair is longer in the center and shaved along the sides in a Mohawk is ridiculous. Now Greg's Mohawk is rubber banded up so that the mohawk will soon be a dreadlock Mohawk. In addition to the rubber banded Mohawk Greg has made horns made of his hair like devil horns. The hair devil horns are molded with gel. It is quite a look. It is as ridiculous as my bald head.

I was disappointed when the grand jury was extended by the Prosecutors but I was not surprised. Federal Grand Juries can sit for 18 months. They can also be extended. Greg and I thought the term of the Grand Jury causing his confinement concluded July 15. If the Grand Jury's term expires then Greg would have to be released by operation of law. Greg and I had fantasized about me picking him up. We imagined that we would walk out of the prison together wearing t-shirts that say CANCER SUCKS. I would be bald, Greg would have his dreadlock Mohawk with horns hair and every newspaper in the country would run that picture. Every television station would play the clip or not play the clip, not because they did not want to, but because they are afraid to because the t-shirts say "Cancer Sucks" and Greg looks like a Rastafarian devil walking with a bald woman. And Barry earns more in a year than most doctors earn in a lifetime. What a ridiculous situation, on all levels.

I cheered when Barry hit the homer. So did Woody. But when I stop and think about Barry's response to the question about Greg I am not cheering. The whole thing is insane. How does one measure the value of a home run? It is not so much that a home run was hit as much as who hit it, at least as it has come to be when Barry Bonds hits one.

Greg sits and Barry hits and there are six weeks left to the season. I have one more chemo treatment. I am going to get Greg out of prison and when that day comes Greg will wear a "cancer sucks" shirt and if I have hair then I will shave my head. It will still be a good picture.

Manaswar may have a torn ACL. That is what the vet said yesterday. Manaswar limps. I have to lift her onto my bed. Now she is sleeping. I love her. I love spending time with her.

On August 9, 2007 President Bush called Barry Bonds to congratulate him for breaking the home run record. That is insane. Perhaps President Bush had forgotten that his US Attorney's Office had caused a grand jury to be convened to investigate Barry Bonds. Maybe he did forget. He has a lot on his mind, a war in Iraq, his Lyme disease, breast cancer-oops that is me. I inquired as to whether Barry addressed the grand jury issue with the President. Apparently he did not as he thought that would have been disrespectful. That is hilarious. It is like Hitler calling Churchill to congratulate him. It is like Osama

Bin Laden's family being escorted out of the United States two days after 9-11 by Bush. Oh wait he did do that. Clearly the President has a problem with boundaries. He loves everybody or maybe he hates everybody. Does he have the power of discernment? So Bush called Barry Bonds. That must have been quite a conversation between the President and the home run King. And I wonder why I have cancer. One would have to be self obsessed to hit a home run. It takes a lot of coordination, practice and concentration to hit a home run. Concentration. 46,000 people screaming, booing, calling, ignoring and the pitcher throws the ball 90 plus miles per hour and the batter swings a wooden bat and tries to hit the ball. So that is what Barry Bonds has done 756 times and a myriad of others for each pitch at each at bat. That takes a lot of concentration. Barry has that. As for the President the fact that he is the President says far more about the failures of the American system than his innate incompetence. As for the baseball system either the batter gets a hit or he doesn't. I like baseball better than politics. Even with performance enhancers baseball seems more fair.

Something is wrong anytime lawyers are involved in games. Games are games and lawyers should stay out of them. George Mitchell the retired Senator should not have been selected to run the investigation. A baseball man should have been selected, an athlete, a player, someone like Lou Pinella. He would say, "all right who used steroids" Then he would scream at them until someone answered. Then he would kick dirt on them and scream some more and then it would be over. That would have been a far more effective way to deal with whatever it is we are dealing with. Any time lawyers get involved the issues get convoluted and procedure becomes bigger than substance. The Federal Government is spending tens of thousands of dollars investigating athletes about what they eat and drink and inject or put under their tongue. Money, money, money spent to look at how a person plays a sport. We are insane. Let baseball people regulate baseball without lawyers.

I feel like shit. Taxol and neupagen…nasty…hurts and pains and now I will nap. I won't dream about lawyers. I won't dream about baseball. I won't dream about money. I just hope to not feel pain.

# 20

# HAS THIS EXPERIENCE CHANGED ME

Saturday August 11, 2007

This morning Woody and I talked about whether or not this cancer/chemo experience had changed us and how. I asked Woody, "Do you think this has changed you?" Woody looked at me with her earnest eyes and answered, "Yes." She paused. I thought Woody was going to tell me that she had learned hope or patience or really felt an improvement in her spiritual life, or some such incredibly meaningful thing. Instead Woody said, "I am more depressed than I have ever been in my life." Then she laughed. I was shocked as much by her words as her laugh. I knew that what she said was true. This has been terrible for Woody. I also know that it is so terrible that it is funny. Being asked by a woman who is experiencing chemically induced baldness whether or not cancer/chemo has changed their lives is really funny.

I do not think that I am more depressed than I have ever been in my life. I think I am happier than I have ever been. I am sorry that Woody is depressed. I think she is depressed but also I think she is not. Maybe she is manic. I am manic. I always have been. So it makes perfect sense that I would have cancer and be doing chemo and be happier than I have ever been. I was happier than I have ever been in my life when I got the diagnosis and I have just gotten happier. I am not happy when I am sick from the chemo. I am not happy when needles and stuff are being stuck in me. But all the rest of the time I am happy. I do not worry as much, but I still worry. I do not know if the diminution of worry is from an evolved state of acceptance or is chemo brain, a warned against consequence of chemotherapy.

Woody and I have spent more time together than we ever have. I have spent more time with the dogs than I ever have. I think they all like it. I have watched more Matlock episodes than I ever have in my life. I love Matlock. I used to love Perry Mason. I still do, but I like Matlock better. I am more like Matlock than Perry Mason when I do cross- examination. I am kind of charming and self-deprecating until I am not and go in for the kill. It is fun to do. But actually it is much easier and thus more fun to just watch Matlock cross examine than to do it myself. It is also far less stressful. Matlock comes on now at 12 p.m. and 1 p.m. Monday through Friday on the Hallmark Channel. (Matlock used to come on at 1 p.m. and 2 p.m.) That worked for me. No matter what I would be home by 1 p.m. or awake by 1 p.m. to watch Matlock. Then somehow some way Matlock would lull me into a state of peace. I would fall asleep and miss most of the episode. Then somehow some way I would wake up about 15 minutes before the end of the show to watch Matlock cross examine a few witnesses, vindicate his client, and catch the real killer. He did all that in 15 minutes. I find that comforting.

Last week they changed the Matlock times back an hour so now he starts at noon. I am having trouble adjusting to the new schedule.

As the days have gone by when I do not work I find myself getting up later and later. I used to get up every morning about 6 a.m., sometimes earlier. Now I get up around 8 a.m. or 9 a.m. because I no longer have to be in Court at 9 a.m. or any time for that matter. 9 a.m. is way too early to start anything. Nothing should start until 10 a.m. People should get to relax and enjoy the day. Court should not take two hours for anything much less three and then lunch and then another three to four hours in the afternoon. Court should be like Matlock, 15 minutes of good cross and be done with it.

The point is that I have enjoyed not working so much. I have enjoyed the time that I have spent thinking about my life. I have lots of great stories and have done so many great things and met so many interesting people that I have a lot to think about. I like thinking and writing and appreciating and laughing about it all. I never would have taken the time to do this if I had not had to do chemotherapy. Not that I had to. I chose to. But I chose to do chemotherapy because I think it was the smart decision. I do want to live and have a good time.

I had to come to terms with myself. I have to be okay with who I am and what I have done and I have to stop worrying. I am typing this. My mother told me never to learn how to type otherwise I would be a secretary and be told what to do all day long. So I did what my mother told me and never learned how to type. Now I am one of the worst typists I know. I wish that I had taken typing. Computers make life easier and typing makes it easier to input the data into the computer. But not learning to type, not knowing how to type really led to a battle with computers. How funny that my mother's solution to avoid being told what to do was to fail to learn how to type. I can sort of type now. I think I could have learned how to type and also learned how to be independent.

I have thought about all the things that I learned. One lesson is knowing how to do something, whatever it is, is always better than not knowing. The correct lesson would have been to learn how to type and learn how to say no. But my mother who by the way is 86 years old and cancer free always tried her hardest to give me the best life possible. No one in my family has ever had cancer. My mother smokes at least three packs of cigarettes day. She always has. My mother looks great for 86. In fact no one believes that she is 86. My mother was in great shape until just a few years ago. Now she has some arthritis and osteoporosis and hurts a lot. But she still smokes.

When I told my mother that I had been diagnosed with breast cancer she looked at me and took a big puff on her cigarette drawing the smoke in. She blew the smoke out saying at the same time, "I can't believe you have cancer." Compared to her, neither could I. A few years ago when my mother was about 82 she had to have an angioplasty or some sort of heart procedure. I took her to the hospital. Her friend Bernice came with us. My mother had to be anesthetized. During the procedure Bernice and I went and looked at new cars. We also went to lunch and had a good time. But all the while I worried that when we got back the doctors would tell me that there was something wrong with my mother's heart. It was a rational concern.

My mother has smoked cigarettes since she was about 20 years old. At the point of the procedure she had been smoking for 62 years. If her smoking was a life she would be eligible for social security. She has smoked several packs a day for her entire life. I vaguely remember a day when I was 10 or 11 that my mother tried to quit. I think she lasted a day. She was grumpy and miserable. I did not notice that she was not smoking. But when she lit up the next day and announced that she was no longer quitting smoking I suddenly understood why she was so jumpy the day before. I encouraged her to smoke.

I started smoking when I was about 12 or 13. My next door neighbor and I would steal our mothers' cigarettes and then we would smoke them. Steven and I met when we were about 8 or 9. We were both born in 1955. He was born in April and I was born in March so I was a month older. Somehow that mattered to me. His father was an officer in the Navy. My father was an officer in the Air Force. Both our mothers' smoked. We played football and baseball and wiffle ball. I was a tomboy. In the winter we would throw snowballs at cars. We never got caught. We liked to throw things.

We would play in the woods and explore. One day for whatever reason we decided to explore deep into the woods. We were about 10 years old. We had my brother Robby with us. Robby was two and half years younger than us. But to Steven and I it felt like a lot more than that and that Robby was just a little kid. I do not know why Robby was with us. We rarely let him play with us. But he was with us. We explored and somehow Robby got scared. I think he thought he saw a snake in a creek. I think it was a stick. But he thought it was a snake and freaked out. I also freaked out even though I did not see a snake and thought it was a stick because I hate snakes.

When I was little girl in England my family went to the London zoo. My family was my mother, my father, my younger brother Robby, and me. I had never been to a zoo before. My mother dressed me up in a nice dress. It was a Sunday. I was about 5 or 6. It was 1960 or 61. The zoo was being rebuilt and replenished. During World War II London was bombed relentlessly and the zoo and its many animals were damaged. So some 15 years after the end of the War the London Zoo was just getting going again. There was a snake pit at the Zoo. It was a big concrete pit with rocks and trees and lots and lots of snakes. Surrounding the pit was a concrete wall and a short fence on the wall. My father decided that I should be able to see the snakes better than my limited view. I did not want to see the snakes better. In fact I had already figured out in my little mind that I had absolutely no desire to see any snakes at all, much less angry snakes stuck in a concrete pit.

My father grabbed me in my nice coat and dress and lifted me up. I was a very little girl so if you found me to grab I was easy to lift up. My father had found me and grabbed me and he lifted me up. I did not say a thing. He lifted me up and over the short fence at the concrete wall and held me over the pit so that I could see the snakes. I did not look at the snakes. I was terrified. I tried not to move or express any sentiment to my father. I did not want him to know I was scared. If he knew, all he would have said was that I had no right to be scared and he would have held me over the snake pit longer. I do not think he was mean, just incredibly insensitive. But it felt mean to me. I stayed as still as I could and hoped that my mother would notice that my father was holding me by my coat over a snake pit before he dropped me and I would be killed by all the snakes biting me.

My mother must have been watching Robby because I remember that Robby was in his stroller. I think my father held me over the pit for about a year before my mother noticed what he was doing. I can still hear her shout at my father, "Bob what are you doing, put Paula down on the ground." My mother had a history of protecting me from my father's reckless behavior. On the ship to England my mother found my father pushing me on a swing on the ship that swung out over the water. I was 4. I was scared but there was no stopping my father from pushing the swing until my mother caught him and yelled, "Bob what are you doing?" No wonder my mother smoked. I would have smoked too if I thought it would help.

We were in the woods and Robby was afraid of the snake that I thought was a stick. We were so lost. At that creek Steven and I got completely disoriented. The whole snake-stick quandary with Robby crying that we were lost got us lost. We walked and walked and ended up several miles from our homes in a neighborhood where we had never been. We randomly picked a house and went and knocked on the door. We told the lady we were lost and asked if we could use her telephone. There were no cell phones back then.

The lady called our mothers and our mothers drove over. They were relieved that we had been found. They were angry that we had gone so far. Robby was still crying. I kind of felt like crying because I was scared. But I did not shed a tear. I pretended I was not scared, only lost. Shortly after that Steven and I started stealing cigarettes from our mothers and went to the woods without Robby and sat and smoked. It seemed safer than exploring.

Steven and I were each hooked by 14. We smoked a lot together. We did all the things that teenagers do together. We drank, smoked pot, took drugs, looked at posters lit only by a black light and listened to Led Zeppelin. For a few years Steven and I were inseparable. Then my family moved when I was 15. We pretty much stopped seeing each other. Our mothers stayed close. They still talk. They are each widows, and have been for about 20 years. I would ask my mother how Mrs. Langley is and how Steven is. There was never much detail. Then a few years ago my mother told me that Mrs. Langley had called and that Steven had died of liver cancer.

I never called Mrs. Langley or his sister and expressed my condolences. I never wanted to acknowledge that Steven had died before the age of 50 of liver cancer. I had planned on calling him and seeing him and talking about our lives and telling him that I really enjoyed all of the things we did together, even all of the bad things, especially all of the bad things. It has only been in the past few weeks that I have even thought about Steven. It really upset me when I heard that he was dead of cancer. It felt like a double whammy- that Steven was dead and that he died of cancer. Both things felt wrong.

Now some five years later I have breast cancer and my mother still smokes as does Mrs. Langley. These two officer's wives in their 80's watching their child go through chemotherapy. Mrs. Langley had to go to Steven's funeral. That must have been really sad for her. I know this is hard on my mother. But I hope I do not die from cancer. I do not want to die any time soon. There are some more things that I want to do. I want to feel good about being me. I want to do what I want to do. I did tell my mother when she exhaled her inhaled cigarette smoke and said that she could not believe that I have cancer that, " I will be goddamned if you will outlive me." We laughed.

When Bernice and I got back from car shopping we waited in the hospital waiting room for word about my mother. As I said, I believe that I had just cause for concern given all the cigarettes my mother had smoked over the course of her life. 68 years worth of 2 to 3 packs a day. That is almost a million cigarettes. Maybe my mother has smoked more cigarettes than any living person. My mother is to cigarettes what Barry Bonds is to home runs. My mother has smoked at least 990,000 cigarettes. No wonder I worry about her heart.

My mother really may have smoked more cigarettes than any living person. My mother should be eligible for the Guinness Book of World Records for most cigarettes smoked by a living person, if they had such a record. She should win a prize. She should be a poster child, actually poster elder for cigarettes. When she smokes one million cigarettes we should have a party and a commemorative ceremony.

Because when Bernice and I got back to the hospital to hear the results of my mother's procedure and hear what I thought for sure would be the dire condition of her heart, nothing happened. We waited and waited. Time dragged, like waiting for a jury time. Powerless time as there is nothing I can do to alter the outcome except wait to hear what the verdict is. The longer I waited for the doctors the worse I thought the news would be.

A doctor came into the waiting room and said my mother was out of surgery, that she was doing well. He asked to speak with me. I stood up. I mustered all my courage. My heart was pounding in anticipation that I would hear terrible news about the smoky condition of my mother's heart. The doctor asked me what kind of cigarettes my mother smoked. He said they all knew about her smoking. They had asked my mother when she started and how much she smokes and the answers amazed the doctors. But the doctors had failed to ask her about the brand. So he asked me rather than wait for my mother to awaken from the anesthesia and ask her himself. I answered, "Marlboro." I then asked what difference the brand she smokes makes.

The doctor answered that he and his colleagues were amazed by the condition of my mother's heart in that it was perfectly healthy, very strong, and could keep on ticking for another 50 years. He said she had the heart of a healthy 40 year old woman. I do not think that is what any of the doctors expected to find. I think they expected to find a small, weak, nicotine filled heart. They got just the opposite. If they had not known they would not have believed that my mother had smoked almost a million cigarettes.

After the medical team finished the procedure to check my mother's heart the doctor and his colleagues offered varying explanations on the amazing condition of my mother's heart. They had no understanding other than to ask the brand she smokes in the hopes that it would lead to some rational explanation. The Doctor said, "Marlboro, hmm, I used to smoke and quit. Marlboro." He smiled and walked away. I imagined him buying a pack of Marlboros on his way home and justifying each puff on my mother's remarkable heart.

Here I am a heretofore healthy and hairy 52 year old woman, now bald and sick from chemotherapy taking care of my 86 year old million cigarette mother. My mother could be the poster child, actually poster elder for the motto, "Cigarettes do not cause cancer." Then me and my bald head could be the poster child- middle-aged poster person (MAPP) for the motto, "Second Hand Smoke Causes Cancer."

It is Sunday. I used to like Sundays. Not because of the church. I stopped that long ago. Not because of not having to go to church because for years I had guilt about not going that made my day worse than an hour in the church. But I have lost the memory of church on Sunday and the guilt that came after. I like pro football. Sunday nights I get nervous because Monday is a workday. I worry about what will happen that next day and all through the week. Now I worry about the nurse who is very good at putting an IV in my arm, putting the IV in my arm. I hate chemo, the process. I hate thinking about it and worrying. I cannot seem to think about things and not worry, at least things like IVs.

# 21

# WHAT AM I GOING TO DO NOW

August 24, 2007

I feel like I have written but according to the computer I have not. The power went out. I am home alone with two dogs and the power went out. Computer by candlelight. How quaint. I called PG and E on my cell phone and complained. I had to use my cell phone because my land phone requires electricity. Electricity would be nice. Could there be cancer without electricity? Certainly without electricity there would be no way to power the diagnostic machines. Well no easy way. Cancer would be like the philosophical question if the tree falls in the woods does it make a sound if no one hears it? If cancer lives in me but nobody finds it does it exist? Does it exist if no one knows it exists? Does it know it exists? Does my cancer exist? Does cancer exist within me? Is it my cancer or is it me or is it not me? Cancer the disease; why does it happen to who it happens to?

Why did this happen to me? Why did my body get cancer? Why did part of my body or all of my body or any of my body make cancer cells? Did my body do it? Did my mind have a part in this? Did my thoughts have a part in what my body did? Why me? And so somewhere in the mix of all of those questions comes the more fundamental individual's existential angst question of who am I?

I think I am my voice. When I think of me I think of my voice. Which part of me is most me? It is no longer my appearance. The bald thing has totally diminished the importance of physical appearance and eliminated my connection to me from my appearance. I am not what I look like. And what I look like is not who I am. Even though it is. It may not be who I think I am. I do not think that I am a bald woman, bald because of chemotherapy, because of breast cancer.

I think somehow part of me thought that because I am a lesbian that I would not get any of the woman related diseases like breast cancer or ovarian cancer. I thought lesbians would only get the gender neutral diseases like the generic body parts i.e. lung, colon etc. Well I was wrong. Imagine that I was wrong about what diseases I would be susceptible to. Not just what diseases I might be susceptible to but also the reason why.

I have blamed a lot on my being a lesbian. Maybe I have been wrong. I have blamed a lot on being raised as a Catholic. Maybe I was wrong. I have blamed a lot on being an alcoholic. Maybe I was wrong. Maybe I have been wrong about a lot of things. I have blamed a lot on myself for having cancer. I have blamed a lot on chemotherapy. I have blamed a lot on other people. I have blamed a lot on institutions. I have blamed outward things because I have difficulty with being me. It is easier to blame others than look at what it is within me that makes me so uncomfortable to be me.

Losing my hair made it very apparent to me that I was not comfortable with my appearance. I have never been comfortable with my appearance. When I realized I was small I was too old not to have understood that I was small. I think I was about 45 when I realized that 5 foot 2 and a half was my size and that such a size is a small size. Even though I was always at the front of the line in grade school some how I never really correlated the fact that I was at the beginning of the line because it was a size ordered line. I was never first in line but always fairly close to the beginning. Kind of like if the line was in alphabetical order and your name began with a c. That is how I saw it.

I weigh about 114 pounds. I think that is big. My dog weighs more than I do. My dog weighs 177. The acupuncture vet today told me Manaswar had to go on a diet. I always try to not get fat. I weigh the same I did for most of my life. I always think I am too fat. I am 52 and I worried about getting fat on chemotherapy. My entire life I have not felt good about my weight. At least I have acknowledged my weight. I ignore my height because if I acknowledge my height, or lack thereof I have to acknowledge that I do not like my height either.

Height is really nothing that I can change. I do wear high heel shoes. I wear heels whether I wear a suit with a skirt or pants. I wear heels because I do not want people to realize how short I am. Some people wear heels for fashion reasons. That is why I think that people think I wear heels, to be fashionable. I wear good clothes to be fashionable and the shoes go with the clothes. Also the two inches of extra height in my mind hides the five pounds that I do not want. Somehow the extra height spreads me out and hides the flaws that I think I am too short and too fat.

Now I think I am too short and too fat and bald. The baldness has distracted me from my height and weight. Being bald is worse than being too short and too fat. I am told that my hair will come back. I could and will lose the pounds. I cannot make myself grow unless I took Human Growth Hormone and I could. I do know where to get it. But HGH causes cancer so I do not want to take that. So I will just wear heels. My height and weight are actually glad that I went bald so that they could have a respite from my constant criticism. I am going to try to stop criticizing myself about my height and weight, especially after I have hair again.

# 22

# DID ANY OF THIS WORK

O n Tuesday August 30, 2007 I had my post chemo MRI. I was nervous and grumpy on Monday and Sunday before testing Tuesday. I was grumpy on Sunday because I was nervous about Monday. Monday I had an infusion of Herceptin, the monocloneoncogene inhibitor. I have no idea what I just said. Because my tumor is her2 positive, the full dose dense chemo regimen includes a year of Herceptin. Genentech makes Herceptin. Genentech holds the patent, a monopoly for about 11 years. One dose of Herceptin costs several thousand dollars. I do not know how that price is determined, certainly not the laws of supply and demand, but probably by the monopoly of patent protection.

There is a huge demand. Maybe not huge but anyone with her2 positive breast cancer ought to want it. My demand was huge. As to supply, only Genentech supplies Herceptin. I have no idea how long it took Genentech to invent Herceptin. I have no idea how much it cost Genentech to invent Herceptin. I imagine that the company has spent a lot of money over the years trying to invent something that makes the her2 oncogene unable to communicate with all the other cells within the body. I am not sure how it works. I do know that it cuts off the ability of the her2 part of a cell to communicate with other cells. I imagine the drug somehow puts duct tape over all the her2 cells in my body so that they cannot recruit the other cells to make cancer cells. Basically Herceptin stops her2's ability to talk.

I think it is very funny that I have a talky tumor, since I have been known to be a talky lawyer. Regardless of what Herceptin is, it is still infused in my body intravenously. The nurses at California Cancer Care are great. They are great at finding a good vein and getting the needle and the tube in my vein that connects to the tube connected to the bag of Herceptin. It is the same every time.

We go to the Cancer Center. We get there. Woody always takes me. Sometimes I drive. Other times Woody drives. If I have smoked pot Woody drives. I rarely smoke pot before an infusion. I think I only did it once. I was not comfortable being high getting an infusion. How ridiculous is that. The one time I did get high Woody and I finished the puzzle in the waiting room of California Cancer Care.

It feels like I have gotten one million infusions. I have only gotten 8 bad chemo infusions and 5 Herceptin infusions. Lucky thirteen, but it does really seem like at least a million. I had bought an outfit for chemo. I stopped wearing it. I decided I did not like it. I no longer wear the same outfit. I wear whatever I feel like wearing. So Woody and I drive there. We go the same way every time- 280 south to 92 to Ralston and at the first 4 way stop after the stoplight we turn into the shopping center with the Safeway, the Starbucks, the pizza place, the Long's Drugs, the butcher, the deli, and the Cancer Center on the second floor. There is an elevator in front of the deli that takes people to the second floor. On the second floor there is a dental office and the Cancer Center, neither choice a good one to me.

When I was a child my mother took me to a dentist. We were in England. She took me to the military dentist at the military base where my father was assigned. I was a little girl, about 4 or 5 years old. The dentist filled a cavity that was in one of my baby teeth. He did not use Novocain. He just drilled and filled. It hurt. I was terrified. But I did not say anything. I did not cry. I just sat there in a big chair designed for big people-adults- and let him drill and fill. Consequently to this day I hate going to the dentist. I cannot seem to erase that one really bad experience from my head. Regardless of who the dentist is, when the dentist says "open your mouth" fear floods my body, sweat starts to pour out of me, and this odd sense of betrayal starts up in my gut. I had trusted my mother. I had trusted the military dentist. So I opened my mouth and then the oblivious sadistic torture started. Why would anyone say to a mother that children do not feel pain and therefore do not require any anesthetic? Why would my mother have believed him? She had been a child. I am not sure that she did believe him. He told her after the fact that he had filled my cavity without Novocain. My mother never brought me back to him again.

When I get off the elevator I go to the Cancer Center not the dentist. And just one other thing regarding me and the military dentist, why would anyone fill a cavity in a baby tooth. The tooth came out a year or two later naturally. I think of the dentist and that experience just about every time I go to the Cancer Center. I never tell anyone bringing me to the Cancer Center, even Woody, about the military dentist and that I would rather be going to the Cancer Center than the dentist. Most every one I have ever ridden with on the elevator up to the second and only floor is going to the Cancer Center. It is easy enough to tell the patients, especially the breast cancer people. We do not have any hair, or very little hair.

For my first round of infusions I went in about noon. That was for the A/C. For the second round of infusions of Taxol/Herceptin I went in about 10 am. The Taxol/ Herceptin takes about 6 to 7 hours. I arrive. I write my name down on the sign in sheet. But the women who run the front desk know almost everyone by name. Marilyn and Marney, whoever is available call back to the infusion center and then one of nurses comes and gets me. The nurses are very busy back there so sometimes it takes a few minutes. The waiting room is large with lots of chairs and magazines and a table that always has a puzzle on it. I try to do the puzzle with Woody. Woody is better at the puzzles than I am except for the day that I smoked pot. I locked in on the puzzle which was close to being finished when we got there that day. We finished it. It was a dachshund in the grass. Funny I finished the puzzle of the dachshund in the grass because I had smoked grass.

Amy is the nurse who helps me. I always pick a room with a bed. There is a big bright and airy room with chairs that I could choose. I never do. I do not want to be sitting up. I do not want to look at others getting infusions or getting stuck with the needle in order to get the infusion. So I pick a room with a bed. The bed I pick is entirely a function of which wrist/arm I want to have the infusion in. Left arm means one side. Right arm means another.

I take off my shoes and lay down. I usually cover my face with a blanket that I bring with me. They have blankets but Marta, my dear friend, gave me a very soft pink blanket and I bring that with me, a security blanket. I cover my head with the blanket and offer up my hand, which ever one it is to be. Amy ties a tourniquet around my arm. We wait for some blood to build up in the chosen vein. Sometimes the vein is on the top of the designated hand, other times it is in the wrist or just below my wrist on my arm. Where ever the designated vein is Amy injects it with some Novocain to numb the area. I do not know how she does what she does because I have never watched. I keep the blanket over my head. She does what she does and in a minute or two she announces "we are in" and that means that something is in my vein that they will attach the tubes of whatever drug or solution they are giving me. Somewhere in that process Amy removes a vile or two of my blood and they run it for my blood counts.

For most of the time my blood counts were acceptable. After the second infusion of Taxol/Herceptin my red blood counts dropped below 10. I think they are normally around 15. At 10 health insurance companies will authorize payment for an injection of a drug called procrit. Procrit increases the production of red blood cells. It is a favorite of world class athletes as the injection causes increased red cell production which allows more oxygen in the blood which translates to better performance. There is also some dispute as to whether or not Procrit stimulates breast tumor growth. My health insurance company had not approved the injection anyway so the point was moot. My other option was a blood transfusion. But that had not been approved either.

Having low red blood cells sucks. It makes me weak and pale. I felt bad. I felt as weak as I was pale. Angela, the Cancer Care nurse practitioner explained that they could not do anything until my health insurance company approved it. She suggested that I wait a week. It would take that long to get the health insurance company's approval. I could wait a week. In that week I would get weaker and weaker as my red blood count declined. I did not want to wait a week.

I called my friend Victor Conte. Victor is the founder of BALCO. Victor is one of the smartest people I have ever met. He knows how to deal with the many mysteries of red blood cells as well as anyone as red blood cells and the blood are so essential to athletic performance. I told Victor the problem about my low red blood count. He came right over in his brand new Bentley and brought me a collection of vitamins and told me when to take what. He brought me vitamin B-12, Vitamin C, Vitamin E, non-constipating iron pills, and folic acid. I did just what Victor said and by the following week my red blood count was back up to ten. Now a few weeks later it is almost to 11. My health insurance company did approve something but I no longer needed it thanks to Victor.

I have called on all the people that I know to help guide me through this process. And people have been amazing. I think the nurses were surprised when I went for chemo the following week and my red blood counts were higher. Amy does not start to run the chemo until the counts are back. If the blood counts are too low they cannot administer the chemo. Mine were always high enough that my chemo regime was always right on schedule. It was close that one time but thanks to Victor's protocol I stayed on schedule.

The protocol is always the same. First comes some saline solution, then antinausea stuff, including steroids, somewhere in there comes the Ativan, then the chemo drugs. The Ativan makes me groggy and often I fell asleep. I was dreamy, sometimes euphoric because of the Ativan. Most times the infusions were uneventful. A few times I got cramping in my veins, a very painful experience. The cramping was caused by some reaction to the antinausea meds so they switched the antinausea med and that did not happen again. I got extra Ativan that one day and had to be led out of the Cancer Center like a drunken sailor.

Every time, 13 times so far and it feels like a million times, is the same. The nurses are really good at what they do. They are by far the best vein finders I have ever seen. For that I am so grateful. I could have had a port put in me. A port is a permanent insertion in a vein. They put this thing in you, usually in the chest, so people cannot see it. And then all the infusions and blood draws are done from the port. I did not want a port and luckily it has not been necessary for me to have one. I do not want a port because I do not want to have to look at it every day. I want to pretend on the days that I do not have chemo or get blood drawn or have some test that none of what is happening is happening. I will put up with the discomfort of the experience time after time rather than live with the constant reminder caused by the port.

And as predictable as the vein finding experience is, and it is predictable, I am as predictable. On Sundays I am grumpy and edgy because I am scared about Mondays and the infusion. But this past Sunday I was grumpy about my Herceptin infusion on Monday and afraid because on Tuesday I had an MRI scheduled.

The MRI is the big ticket item in terms of diagnostics. The work order for the MRI read "evaluate extent of disease in left breast." Above the order was the stated diagnosis of "left breast cancer". There it was-"evaluate extent of disease." I took that to mean did the chemotherapy shrink the tumor. By all accounts the tumor in my left breast had shrunk. Brad, my oncologist said so when he felt my left breast. Lora Burke, my breast surgeon and Dulcy Wolverton, the radiologist had both said so after an ultrasound a few weeks ago. Nevertheless the MRI is the big ticket item. So I was worried that it might not be good enough, that what everyone had felt and saw was somehow wrong. A real possibility to me as to me it still seems so wrong that I had breast cancer to begin with.

# 23

# WHAT TO DO INSTEAD OF WORRYING ABOUT AN MRI

R ather than have a relaxing morning on the Tuesday before my 1 p.m. MRI I went out to Dublin Federal Prison to see Greg Anderson. I had not seen him in about 8 days and that is too long. Traffic driving out there was terrible and that got me agitated. When I got to the prison I realized all of the guards were new. There are the two prisons and an honor camp out there and the administration occasionally reassigns the guards to different facilities. The new guards did not know me. I did not know them.

Before my cancer diagnosis when I went to the prison during the work week I only wore Escada suits. On the weekends I wore shorts, not Escada. Somehow that struck me as powerful, Escada during the week and non-Escada shorts on the weekends. Even people who wear Escada can get cancer, so maybe Escada has only limited power. Since I started chemo and lost my hair I do not wear fancy clothes out there at all. I wear gap khaki pants and a white t-shirt and a button down collar Ralph Lauren shirt, either white or blue pin stripes, and tennis shoes. On my head I wear a blue bandana tied like a pirate. I still carry a long yellow legal pad. That is how they know I am a lawyer.

Greg has been in prison so long he is kind of famous within the prison. Before he was famous because of his stand and imprisonment, Greg was known because he is a great trainer. Greg was Barry Bonds trainer. Greg was many peoples' trainer. Greg is more than a trainer. Greg is a mentor and a motivator. Not many people stand on their principle. That in and of itself adds to the aura of Greg at the prison. I hope I have added to the mystery of Greg by switching from a bleached blonde in Escada to a gap khaki bald woman, sporting a Pirates of the Caribbean bandana do. I go out there at least once every week.

I was surprised by the new group of guards. That gave me something else to worry about, about how long it would take to get in to see Greg, about how long it would take them to bring Greg out to see me. The prison has reassigned guards two prior times. With each of the prior personnel changes came a change in procedure. The first time was last August. I went to see Greg. I was wearing long shorts. They fell below my knee. They were the same shorts I had worn each of the many times I had been out there (washed after each trip to the prison). When I got to the door in my long shorts the guards would not let me in to the prison. These new guards said that shorts were not allowed. I argued. A supervisor came over. The supervisor said there had been a rule change and shorts were no longer allowed. I asked what to me seemed like a reasonable question, "How would I know that."

The supervisor explained that since that was the rule that was the rule and since I knew now that was the rule I would not be admitted into the prison because I was not wearing permissible clothing. I tried to reason with him. I suggested that most skirts are shorter than the shorts that I was wearing. He said that may well be true but that I was wearing shorts that were not allowed as opposed to a short skirt which would be allowed. I lost the argument. I left the prison. I went to a store and bought a pair of camouflage combat pants, put them on, and returned to the prison. Instead of looking like a yuppie lawyer now I looked like a commando. When I returned to the prison I thanked the guard for encouraging me to get the great new pants that I was now wearing. Believe me the shorts were better.

The second rule change that came with the change of personnel was hardly as dramatic but equally annoying. It had to do with the check in procedure. That procedure change, like the day about the shorts, came on a Sunday. After the second rule change on a Sunday I stopped going out to the prison on Sundays. There is no one in real authority out there to control the arbitrary imposition of rules by the guards.

During the work week the procedures are the same even with different guards. The new guards were nice enough. They always are. But they run at their own time and have their own schedules. Attorney visits are not in their routine. Attorneys are an interruption to the tedium of the day. I would think that any interruption would be welcomed. Some do. Others don't. As with all things attitude is everything. Apparently so are routines.

The weekday routine is the same. I walk in the door into a secure room that looks suspiciously like a fish bowl. I push an intercom button, wait to hear a beep, and then I announce myself. I do it the same way every time. I want to have a routine too. I say, "My name is Paula Canny, I am an attorney and I am here to see my client Greg Anderson." They answer by telling me that they will be with me in a minute. It is rarely a minute. Sometimes it has been a lot of minutes.

Since my cancer diagnosis I stopped wearing a watch so I do not stress so much about how long I am waiting because I no longer know. I think it is better that way.

While I wait for a guard to come and get me I fill out a form. I always complete the form before any one comes for me. I must provide my name, business address, make and model and license plate number of my car on the form. The form then asks me to swear that I am not carrying any guns, weapons, or drugs or if I am under the influence of any drugs. I always answer no. I briefly worried about the veracity of the answer to that question, especially since I have been sick and bald from chemo drugs but I hardly think that is what the question is after.

I wait. A guard comes and another guard in the control room remotely unlocks the door and I am let into the vestibule of the prison. I give the guard the form. The guard produces a book from the desk drawer next to the metal detector. The book is the Attorney Visitor's Log. I know that the US Attorney's Office calls the prison and asks who visits Greg. They can call and ask about any inmate. They rarely do. But they do about Greg because Greg is special. The prison provides the answer to them. The guards have told me so.

I fill out the Attorney Visitors Log by writing my name, Greg's name and his inmate number 93389-011, the date and the time. Then I sign the form. I give the guard my driver's license and my California State bar card. The State Bar now provides plastic cards that look like credit cards. But for many years the card was a paper card. The credit card bar card looks much more official. It costs me about $700.00 per year to get the card. I get the card when I pay my mandatory State Bar dues. With that card and a photo id I can get into any jail in the State. For me that is all it is good for.

The guard in the control room keeps my bar card and my driver's license while I see Greg. The guard processing me takes the cards and gives them to the guard in the control room through a retractable drawer like what banks used to use when there were drive through windows, before ATMs.

I empty my pockets and put the contents on the desk. No sunglasses are allowed. No brief cases are allowed. No cell phones are allowed. Computers are not allowed, nor are tape recorders. Practically everything is prohibited. I only bring pleadings and a long yellow legal pad. I bring a lot of change so that I buy treats for Greg from the vending machines. I drop lots of quarters on the desk. Then I walk through the metal detector. If it does go off I walk through a second time and if it does not go off I am ready for the next step.

When I wore Escada I had to take my shoes off because my fancy shoes (always with heels) set off the metal detector. My Nikes do not, so I can leave my tennis shoes on and safely walk through without setting off the metal detector. The first time I went out to the prison after I lost my hair I worried that the guards would make me take off my bandana. I was afraid that I would feel ashamed or that they would ask me to do that to shame me. They did not. That day the guard was so nice I felt cared for. His mother had cancer, so he knew.

The next step is the hand stamp step. The guard stamps my hand. Again it is my choice as to which hand to have stamped. The guard squirts some solution on the pad. The pad is usually dry because it is not used very much as there are not a lot of visitors. The guards call the solution bug juice because it stinks like RAID or some kind of chemical bug killer. It probably causes cancer and I doubt that it has been tested by the FDA. The guard stamps the pad and then my hand. My hand smells like bug juice. Just before I enter the visitor area I place the hand that has been stamped with the bug juice in front of a black light and the bug juice comes up as infrared on my hand. The control room guard sees that I have been stamped with bug juice. The control room guard then remotely unlocks another door and I am permitted to enter the visitor's area.

I waited in the visiting room that Tuesday just like every visit. Some days I wait longer than others. This Tuesday was a long wait. The quarters are for the vending machines. There were 4 vending machines when I started coming some ten months ago. But two machines were taken away, the coffee/ hot chocolate machine and the microwavable food machine. That happened months ago. On my first visit since their removal I asked the guard about the machines. I asked why the machines had gotten to be released. He had no answer. He did not even get the joke. So now there are just the two vending machines. Somewhere in the last six months the change machine was also released so now I make sure I have lots of quarters.

I wait. I buy Greg a bottle of water and a Mother's cookies packet of two oatmeal cookies. Even in prison Greg still eats right. There is a clock in the visitor's room so my watch trick does not work. The clock kept staring at me telling me how long it is taking the guards to get Greg. Eventually Greg is brought in. We visit but I am nervous about the MRI and that I am already late for my doctor's appointment before the MRI. Almost as soon as I get there Greg and I begin the process of my leaving. But these are new guards and it takes about 20 minutes to get out of the visiting area. A guard has to come to get me. No one came for fifteen minutes. The clock told me how long it was taking.

Every time I leave I hug and kiss Greg goodbye. I tell him I love him and mean it as much as I do anything. I leave and I miss him. I walk as fast as I can to my car parked some 100 yards away as they moved the visitor parking lot away from the prison. I always look back. Greg cannot see me. None of the inmates can see out to the parking lot.

The prison was designed that way. There is barbed wire and razor wire around the prison fence and on the walls. The absurdity of housing one of the kindest nicest people in the world behind walls surrounded by razor wire is so perfectly American in this time in America's life. It is as crazy as all the Americans who have cancer.

We have talked Greg and I about the meaning of life and the existential angst. We have pondered why all of what has happened has happened and wondered why he is caught in the middle of this absurd endeavor of attempted coercion. We do not have an answer. To that or to why I got cancer. We also talk about time.

There are so many ways to look at time. I know a day at a time from Alcoholics Anonymous, which is also how I know an hour at a time or a minute at a time. I quit drinking a day at a time. I have been able to not drink for just one day, for days totaling almost twenty one years. When I first arrived at Betty Ford's in 1986, I worried about what I would do at New Years some two and a half months away. I worried how I would ever be able celebrate a birthday or any event without drinking. I worried about what I would say to other people. I worried about excuses. I was so far ahead of myself.

I learned to do my not drinking just one day at a time. I learned I would not drink if all that I had to do was get through one day without drinking. I also learned to just not have any drinks. As long as I do not have one drink I cannot get drunk. I finally understood it is the first drink that gets me drunk. So by not having one drink I have been able to not get drunk. I had lost the ability to control my drinking if I have ever had such ability. When, I am not sure. But I would say by my late twenties, rather than an occasional binge drunk, I was drinking every day fairly heavily, anywhere from 6 to 15 beers a night along with some occasional pot and sometimes cocaine. I was not a drug addict. I am an alcoholic who would do anything to improve my drinking, including taking drugs. I drank to feel better. But over time drinking did not make me feel better. But I kept drinking not to feel better and not to feel worse. At first I drank to feel something. But over the years I drank to not feel anything. It did not work. Not even drinking could take away how much I hated my drinking. It got to the point that I could not pretend anything other than I hated my drinking. My solution, i.e. drinking, had become my problem. And I hated myself.

I did not understand any of that back then some 21 years ago. It has taken 21 years of not drinking a day at a time and four months of chemotherapy for me to truly understand a day at a time. I cannot say that all of that has helped with my attitude towards myself, but it has not hurt. This has not hurt. Writing has helped. Telling the truth helps to be at peace with the truth, whatever it is. That is some of what Greg and I talk about.

Greg and I have a friend named Dot. Dot has done a lot of time, a colloquialism for being incarcerated. Dot has taught us both that when it comes to doing time there are only two days to do- the day you go in and the day you get out. So to do time one should only think about those two days. That way there are only two days to do. So Greg does not do any time. And until the day comes when he gets released he has nothing to do except to wait to do that other day, the day he gets out.

When I left the prison on MRI Tuesday I went to Dr. Martinet's office. JP Martinet is one of the smartest most intuitive people I know. He is a chiropractor. He is also a kinesiologist. He can tell things about my body without a machine that I did not know and that no machine could tell. He makes me feel better. I was late for that appointment. That made me anxious. I did my footbath. I put my feet in some hot water which has an ionizer attached to it sending ions through the water. After 30 minutes in the water my feet are soaked and the water is orange and black and filled with all the materials that have oozed from feet into the water. JP then saw me. He made some adjustments to me and then I was out of there and off to the MRI.

I did more in the morning and early afternoon of that day than I had done all summer, all because I was scared about the MRI. That is what I do. I keep myself busy so that I will not have a feeling, especially a feeling as uncomfortable as fear. I need to change that. I knew that when I planned Tuesday, that I should change my plans to allow for more relaxation. I could have gone to meditate. I could have taken a walk. But both of those things left too much room for feelings. Next time I will pray.

# 24

# THE MRI

St Luke's is the hospital that Dr. Burke, Dr. Wolverton, and Dr. Bourgault work. St Luke's is the hospital where most of my diagnostic tests have been done. It is at the corner of Cesar Chavez and Guerrero Street in the Mission District of San Francisco. It is where I would get the MRI. I found a place to park for free. That was a good sign. I went into the Registration Office and did not have to wait. That was a good sign. I found Woody after I registered and we went and had a bite to eat. We went to the second floor and got off the elevator. As Woody and I walked down the hall we saw Stephanie, the bass player in Woody's band. We were as surprised as Stephanie was to see us. We chatted in the hallway.

As we chatted I looked down the hallway and saw Dr. Lora Burke walking down the hallway. She was wearing blue scrubs. She looked so doctorly and so innocent at the same time. She looked so professional and competent. When I saw her I took that as a good sign. I whistled a wolf whistle at her and she looked up, laughed, and came down the hall. That too was a good sign. A minute or two later Dr. Michelle Bourgault walked down the same hallway that Stephanie and Lora had walked. She joined us. The five of us had a spontaneous party and that was a good sign.

I left the spontaneous hallway party early because I had a 1 p.m. appointment with the MRI machine. I was happy to see the MRI tech. I had done the test four months earlier in May. He gave me the gowns and took me to the locker room and handed a small cup to me with a lid. I asked him what the cup was for. He said, "jewelry". I said, "oh yea, for a moment I thought you wanted me to pee in the cup." When he had handed me the cup that is what I thought- that I had to pee in a cup in a room without a toilet. I was that scared about the MRI that I thought he wanted me to pee in a little cup in a room without a toilet.

I took off my clothes except for my clean good underpants. I put on the hospital gowns. I had forgotten that I had to put on two gowns. I went out to the test room. He gave me the instructions. I did as instructed and lay on the gurney on my back. He gave me the earplugs, orange earplugs and I put them in my ears. He left me alone in the MRI machine room and remotely moved the gurney into the cylinder and the testing began. I had forgotten the noise. I had forgotten almost the whole first test. As I lay on my back trying to be as still as possible with the machine banging, repeatedly banging rapid fire gunshots of sound taking pictures of my innards I lay there wondering why I had not remembered the noise or the closeness of quarters or that the cup was for my jewelry not to pee in.

After about 20 minutes of testing the tech came back into the room and caused the gurney to move out of the cylinder. I had to get up and take off one of the gowns. Then he put an IV in one of my arms. I picked my right arm. He did a good job getting the vein. This time I lay face down on the gurney. They had placed a two holed breast holder on the gurney so that when I laid down each breast got to dangle down in the respective breast holder. I had forgotten that as well. Back in the tube I went. The machine gun banging started again for about 45 minutes off and on. I had forgotten that as well. I thought about the past 4 months. I stayed still a minute at a time and then it was over. When the gurney was remotely removed from the cylinder I bounced up. I looked across the room and saw my reflection in the glass.

I saw myself. I did not see my short self or my too fat self. I saw my bald self, dressed in a hospital gown with orange ear plugs sticking out of my ears. I did not see myself as myself. I saw one of the rubber squeeze dolls that when squeezed the eyes and ears pop out. My eyes had popped out when I saw my bald self with the orange ear plugs sticking out. I could not believe that was me, that any of this was me. And then I totally accepted that it was me. I looked ridiculous. Then I said to everyone including Mary who had come over from radiology to visit, all that I just wrote. They all agreed that I looked like that rubber squeezy doll. We all had a good laugh.

In spite of my outward good nature inside I was grumpy and nervous and in spite of my best intentions I was worried. Had any of this worked? Was I now riddled with cancer? What was going to happen? Would my left breast get to stay with the rest of us?

On Wednesday afternoon Dr. Lora Burke called me and left me a message that the MRI was good, that my tumor was smaller, that she and Dulcy were pleased. Brad had been pleased as well a few weeks earlier. Now I was pleased as well. The chemotherapy had worked. It had shrunk the tumor in my left breast. Goodbye tumor. Hello left breast. I love my left breast. I am attached to my left breast. I am so relieved that my left breast and I will live happily ever after. I suppose loving my left breast is a step in the right direction towards self love. I worry that what I call self love may be nothing more than vanity. I did chemotherapy because I did not want to be lopsided. I was worried about how I would look in my clothes and bathing suits and gym clothes without my left breast. I know reconstruction is available. It was and still is. But I wanted my left breast.

# 25

## CHOICES

When Dr. Burke was still only Dr. Burke to me, when we first met, Dr. Burke explained the options to me about my left breast. That was some four months ago. I could not even take in what she was saying. I pretended like I could. I pretended that I understood what she was saying to me. Woody was there. I am not sure whether or not Woody understood. I am not sure whether or not Woody understood that I was pretending to understand as Dr. Burke explained the various surgical options to remove the cancer in my left breast.

Option one was to do a lumpectomy, which means removal of the cancerous lump, the tumor. Whether or not a lumpectomy was a viable option depended upon the size of the tumor. At our first meeting we did not really know how big the tumor was or if the cancer was any other place in my body.

Option two was to do a mastectomy, meaning remove my left breast. A mastectomy required further choices like whether or not to have reconstructive surgery and if so what kind. Dr. Burke explained all of the choices and the variants of reconstruction. All I heard was that she cuts my stomach muscles or some other body part and makes them into a breast. That may not be what she said. In fact I am sure that is not what she said. But it is what I heard.

I knew I wanted my stomach muscles to stay being my stomach muscles. I had not done 40 years worth of sit-ups to turn them into a breast. I know there are the silicon implant options. At least I save my stomach muscles. I think I told Dr. Burke on that first day with all the bravado that a petrified control freak could muster, "Maybe I should just chop them off." In my absolute ignorant panic I was prepared to give up not just my left breast but my right one as well. My right breast that had made the cyst to make the bump that would make me go to the doctor's to find the cancer in my left breast. That is hardly the treatment that my heroic right breast deserved.

Instead of treating my right breast as the life saving hero that she is I was prepared in that crazy scared moment to have her lopped off. Luckily Dr. Burke suggested that I take some time to think about what to do as well as gather more information.

I imagined some kind of breast removing guillotine. That was what my head thought. That some how my breasts, the both of them, were some kind of culprits deserving of execution. My head screamed, "Off with the breasts." This is the same head that told me to drink and drink and drink and landed me in Betty Ford's. My mind is a very dangerous place and I should not be left alone with it. I know that about my mind so I am vigilant about me watching me. I have the help of many friends and in this instance I also have the help of great doctors.

139

When I got the biopsy results back and learned that the tumor was an aggressive type of cancer that chemotherapy would best address, the choice of what route to take became clearer in my mind. Chemotherapy before surgery would hopefully shrink the tumor and then require only a lumpectomy to remove the shrunken tumor. If I had the surgery before the chemotherapy how would I know that the chemotherapy had even worked? By doing chemotherapy before the surgery, whatever type I chose, I could see for myself what the chemotherapy had done to the cancer. That was and is important to me.

I am glad that the tumor has shrunk. I am glad that the chemotherapy worked. All of this feels tenuous. I am scared that the cancer will come back. I am scared that I will have to go through more chemotherapy at some point. I am scared that I would make that choice again. I am scared that the chemotherapy has done things to other parts of my body that I have yet to even discover. I am scared that the solution may create problems. I have had that experience so it is a fair concern.

# 26

# WHEN SOLUTIONS BECOME PROBLEMS

I have fuzz on my head. I think it is white fuzz. I asked God for hair and forgot to specify color. I had thought about a request for a specific color and decided against such a request of God. Any hair is good hair. I am not sure what white fuzz will translate to but Marta told me that is what product is for as well as hair salons. I just want them to have something to work with. But the same issue of a solution becoming a problem arises. I do not want to put a product on my hair that is on my head that could possibly cause any problems for my body.

The cancer was the problem-is the problem. My body made some cancer. I am very lucky in that the place that cancer decided to live is my breast. I am lucky that I do not have pancreatic cancer, colon cancer, lung cancer. I suppose if one must have cancer a breast is the least bad place. But why did I get cancer in my left breast? What did

I do to my body to have cancer in my left breast? What did I put in my body to have cancer in my left breast? What have I been around or been exposed to have cancer in my left breast? Cancer just does not show up for no reason. There is some reason. I just do not know what it is.

So the chemotherapy was the solution for the cancer. But I am not so sure that the problem is the cancer. I think the problem is in my immune system and in me that allowed the cancer to grow and flourish. People of my generation have been exposed to more toxic substances than persons of any other generation. I have ingested more nitrates, preservatives, hormone fed, steroid injected food products than persons of any other generation. All of that food consumed by my generation has been manufactured and approved by the United States Government's Food and Drug Administration.

How did that come to be that the same bureaucracy regulates food and drugs? How would anyone believe that drugs and food are rationally related? They are not. I think of food as something that is grown. I think of drugs as something that is man made. Maybe there is a connection. The Food and Drug Administration regulates man made food and man made drugs. But why should we make food. Why would anyone make hamburger helper? All of the manufactured food that is regulated by the FDA cannot be good for anyone even if it has the FDA's seal of approval.

We have choices. I have a choice about what I eat. I have a choice about what I buy to eat and where I buy it. I actually have never bought hamburger helper. I am not sure that I have knowingly eaten it. I have never understood my aversion to large mega supermarkets until now. It is not the size of the store that bothers me. It is that the store is filled with manmade nitrate and corn syrup filled manufactured food that is dangerous. Talk about a quality of life conundrum. My life is easier because I can buy FDA approved manufactured food that contributes to the immune system overload that I have subjected my body to. But who knew.

I did not know. I had never really thought about any of this. I thought because I worked out and had strong muscles that this would never happen to me. If cancer can happen to me it can happen to anyone. Anything that can happen to someone can happen to anyone. The anyones and the someones of cancer are growing and growing and cancer has happened in one form or another to every American. I have to make changes in my life so that I reduce my exposure to the many poisons that are passed off as FDA approved.

I worry about cell phones, not the phones themselves but the electronic impulses all around me. My skin was not designed to protect me from cell phone signals and wifi and satellite dish signals. All of these signals must be doing something to us all. How could they not. Our technology has grown faster than my body's ability to adapt to protect itself from the technology. I think that is true and I am afraid that it is true. Yet I talk on my cell phone and have wifi set up in my house and I ate hot dogs with nitrates and baked beans sweetened with corn syrup and I wonder why I have cancer. Perhaps the better question is why don't more people have cancer? Oh wait they do. More and more people have cancer. People are getting cancer younger and younger. It is an epidemic. And it took my right breast to tell me about my left breast for me to understand that anyone, including me, can get cancer.

I understand far more than I ever expected to understand. I understand my choices as they relate to my left breast. I choose to keep my left breast. I am lucky that I have the luxury of that choice. I am lucky in so many ways. I am still scared. I still wonder if I am making the right the decision. I am committing to more mammograms. I am committing to caring for my breasts. I am committed to worrying about my breasts and dealing with the fact that as long as they are on me I must know that cancer could return and then once again all that has happened will happen except that I could have a mastectomy and live the rest of my days without my unlucky breasts.

# 27

# TEMPER TANTRUMS

September 7, 2007

I get so angry sometimes. I have been back to work for all of two days. I have lost my temper at least 25 times over the past two days. The best part of being sick from chemo was that I did not lose my temper. I loved not losing my temper. I am not sure I even realized how nice it was for me not to lose my temper. Yesterday when I went to the office for the first time since my last bad chemotherapy I lost my temper while driving to the office. I was talking on the cell phone on the way to my office and I lost my temper. I yelled at the person on the other cell phone that I was talking with. I got angry with that 'self righteous I am right anger'. Before I knew it I had lost my temper, which ironically meant I found my temper that during chemotherapy I had lost.

My temper is back. Just the thought of the stress of work and I am right back to my worst self. I am so disappointed with myself. I expected more of myself. I thought that I had learned something from chemotherapy, not from the chemo itself but from the time of not working. I had day after day to reflect upon my life. One of the many things that I reflected about was that I would not lose my temper. I may not have said it before, but I swear I thought that I would not lose my temper any more.

I do not know what causes cancer. I do not think that the adrenalin rush of a temper tantrum infuses my body with good feelings. I scare the dogs. I scare whoever. I think the temper tantrums scare the nontantrumming cells in my body. It cannot be good for me. I know that it cannot be good for me and yet I do it. That is nothing new. I have done so many things in my life that I knew were not good for me. Until the point that I stopped, I felt powerless to stop. Drinking was one such behavior. Losing my temper is not a feeling. It is a behavior. The rush that comes from the crescendo of enraged temper loss is much like the rush of warmth that would come when I drank or the rush that would come when I snorted cocaine.

I do not want to lose my temper anymore. I cannot stop working. Maybe I can. Work may be a trigger to losing my temper, but I am responsible for my temper. I should not blame work. I should not blame other people for my losing my temper. And that is what I do. That is what I did. I do not want to do it anymore.

In two days I have seen the oncologist, the breast surgeon, the acupuncturist, the pre-op people, had some blood drawn, had an EKG, worked about 10 hours, went to an AA meeting, and screamed at anyone I could scream at. I do not think that is the best way for me to behave, nor can it be good for the objects of my anger.

The people I love the most stress me out the most. I worry about my mother. She may still smoke two packs a day but she has a lot of health problems and she is 86. I worry that someone is going to knock her over and that she is just going to crumble. Her osteoporosis is terrible and she is disintegrating. I worry about her. I worry that she is in a lot of pain, which she is. I feel powerless and that makes me angry. I am powerless about a lot of what goes on in my life. That is nothing new. But having cancer and having needles put in my veins and just having the cancer itself is a stark reminder that I am powerless. At the same time I am powerful. I have the power to choose. I have the power to choose how I behave. Yet somehow I lose my temper. Even the choice of the word "Lose" connotes that it, my temper, is an act of negligence rather than a purposeful act. It is a purposeful act.

I worry about how I am going to support my mother. I worry about my mother's quality of life. My mother has helped me for years, in so many ways and in so many things. I have helped my mother back for years. My father was a Colonel in the United States Air Force. He retired from the Air Force when I was in eighth grade. There was a small ceremony at the Pentagon. I remember the day vividly. I wore a dress, and not my school uniform. It was a big enough day that I left school early to change my clothes for the ceremony. My brother left school early as well and he wore a coat and tie. My mother looked really great. My father wore his uniform. He looked impressive and important.

An Air Force Officer's uniform is impressive. It is blue, a rich Air Force blue. Officers wear bars on the shoulders to show rank. On the chest are the ribbons that signify medals awarded for bravery or being wounded or a specific skill. My father had lots of ribbons. He looked important in his uniform.

My father drove to the Pentagon. Just like always we drove in the family car, a Buick Le Sabre. My Mother sat in the front passenger seat. My brother and I sat in the back seat. No one wore seat belts. In the late sixties cars were equipped with seat belts but no one wore them. That is really very funny. It took laws to get us to wear seat belts.

My mother smoked cigarettes. My father smoked a cigar. My brother and I tried to breathe. Everyone was nervous. When everyone or anyone was nervous in our family it was safest to be quiet. Otherwise there would be a shouting, screaming fight. So we rode in silence in the car to the retirement ceremony.

When we got to the Pentagon my father did not know exactly where to go. He did not say that. He pretended he knew where he was and what he was doing. The Pentagon is shaped just like what it sounds, a pentagon. The point being if a person enters the building in the wrong door it could be a long walk to the right door. My father knew that much. There was also not a lot of parking. Actually there was lots of parking but all of the places were filled. There were lots of cars. In fact there were more cars than there were parking places. My father drove us around in the Buick Le Sabre looking for a parking place, waiting for someone to leave the lot. It was getting close to the time his ceremony was to begin. Everyone was on edge, except maybe my brother because he was the happiest little boy, oblivious to everything and happy.

A parking place opened up. My father saw the car leaving the parking place. We were in another aisle. He sped up and turned the corner to the aisle with the now vacant parking place. Another car also looking for a parking place also saw what my father saw. The other car headed for the vacant parking place and pulled into the space just before my father could. My father started screaming at the man who stole his parking place. My father lost his temper. When the man started walking towards the building entrance my father continued to yell at the man. The man kept walking. Then my father got quiet. We all were quiet. As the man approached the building entrance about 50 yards from where he had stolen my father's parking space, just where the aisle opens to the road, my father floored the car.

My father literally put the pedal to the metal. My father made the Buick Le Sabre take off so fast that my head jerked back. My Mother yelled, "Bob, what are you doing?" I knew. I did not need to ask. The car increased speed. The man did not hear us coming at first. He had walked away without responding to my father's obscenities. I think he thought it best to avoid eye contact with my father who was clearly enraged. He could have given up the parking place. He should have. We had been there far longer than he had. I do believe that he had stolen our parking place. I do not think that is how he saw it. I think he thought he was just lucky. But when the Buick Le Sabre came driving towards him at however fast the car could go with the pedal to the metal I don't think he felt so lucky. My mother yelled at my father to stop. There was no stopping my father.

The man jumped out of the way. We did not hit the man because the man jumped out of the way. I do not know if my father would really have hit him. I think so. I do not remember finding a parking place. We did. All I could think about was the look on the man's face and the sound of my mother yelling at my father to stop.

We went to the retirement ceremony. It was all very ceremonious. None of us spoke about the man who stole our parking place. I worried that we would run into him in the Pentagon. I worried during the whole ceremony that someone would come get us all for trying to run over the man who stole our parking place. I did not pay attention to the pomp and circumstance of the ceremony. I only hoped that it would end soon enough so that we could leave and get out of there without any further incidents.

I have since discussed the situation of that day with my mother two times. She smoked when we spoke about it the first time. That was years ago and well before my cancer diagnosis. The first time we spoke about the incident was about a year after my father died. My father died of a heart attack almost twenty years ago. He was 67. He was at home and had chest pains. He put out his cigar and drove to a health care clinic in the shopping center closest to my parents' house. I visited the doctor that ran the clinic so he could tell me what happened.

It was October 3, 1988 late in the morning. My father walked into the clinic at about 11 a.m. clutching his chest. Almost as soon as he walked into the door my father dropped dead on the floor of the clinic just in front of the receptionist area. The receptionist called for the doctor. Everyone came running. They tried CPR. They called an ambulance. My dad never really came to again. He died that morning. It was a complete shock to me. My then law partner came to court to tell me. He told me. I did not believe it. I felt numb and shocked. I left the courthouse and drove to my parents', well now just my mother's house at Lake of the Pines in between Auburn and Grass Valley in the gold country just north of Sacramento.

About a year after my father died I asked my mother about my father's retirement, and about the events leading up to it. In the year since my father died my mother and I came to realize that when my father retired he had filled out paperwork regarding his retirement options. My mother did not really know that was what he had done. She vaguely recalled that he had completed forms. What neither of us realized was that when he filled out the forms he checked off the box that allowed him to collect a slightly higher monthly retirement check but that the bulk of the stipend would terminate upon his death. In other words once he died there would be virtually no retirement check for my mother. It took my mother and I a year to figure out what he had done and why my mother was not getting any more retirement checks.

It was in that context that I asked her about the parking lot incident. My mother smoked as we talked. She had no idea when he completed the forms. She did not say much about the matter other than, "If your father were alive I would kill him." She blew smoke out of her mouth when she said it. That is how I knew she was really mad.

I do not blame her for being angry. I still am. I am angry every time that I give a check to my mother. My father should have checked the other box. He should have checked the box that allowed the retirement to continue after his death. That was my father.

My father raged. I worry that I am like him sometimes in my temper tantrums. I believe I have better judgment. I would have checked the box that allowed retirement to continue past my death. But still I have temper tantrums. And I support my mother and have for some twenty years and I always will, just like she has always taken care of me. And I am glad of both things. I just wish that I would not have temper tantrums.

# 28

# THE EASY DOES IT LAWYER

I have not had any chemo for twenty days. I have fuzz on my head.
I feel better physically. I played golf today. I will have surgery on
Thursday. None of those things has made me angry. I have not
had a temper tantrum about any of those things.

On the other hand I have worked for the past several days and had
at least twenty temper tantrums at work. The best part about chemo
was not working and not having temper tantrums. I know it is
counter productive to have tantrums. I know that tantrums do not
help anything. Knowing that and stopping the behavior are different.
I am just not sure how to stop my tantrums.

I came to understand that if I had one drink, I would have another
and another and some days more others and some days not so many
more. I got to the point with my drinking that getting drunk did not
feel good. But still I did it anyway. I just did it, a drink at a time. I
knew I was an alcoholic. When I was 25 I went to AA meetings and

hated them. I felt filled with shame. My ears would turn red I felt so much shame. Of course at the time that I felt those feelings I had no idea what I was feeling. I just knew that I felt uncomfortable and that my ears turned red. I blamed the whole set of uncomfortable feelings on the meeting.

In those days I would go to an AA meeting and feel so terrible about being at the meeting that I would leave the meeting and drink far more than if I just skipped the meeting and tried to control my drinking. After repeated instances of attending AA meetings and getting absolutely shit faced drunk after them I decided that I had to stop going to those meetings because they made my drinking so much worse. I decided there was nothing wrong with being an alcoholic that a drink would not cure. I did not want to be a sober alcoholic. I could not imagine not drinking. I certainly did not practice not drinking. Instead I practiced drinking until I went to Betty Ford's some six years later.

I practiced drinking and trying to control my drinking. Towards the end I did not really try to control my drinking so much as I tried to control how many people knew I was drinking as much as I was. I isolated and did not make telephone calls. Those late night phone calls are a clear indicator that the caller is drunk. I did not go out. I bought my beers from one of my neighborhood stores, varying store from night to night. I drank them home alone. When I went out I did not drink much. I came home early so I could drink comfortably the way I wanted and not worry about what other people thought when I had maybe my thirteenth beer, or my fourteenth beer. I did not have to worry about slurring my speech or staggering or spilling. It was just me and my beer.

Then that was not enough. Or perhaps it was too much. I stopped drinking. I really let it go completely. I have not had a drink since I went to Betty Ford's. I have wanted to get drunk. But I just have not had a drink because I cannot control my drinking. I do not want to go back to that state. It was terrible.

That is kind of how I feel about my temper tantrums. But I don't have temper tantrums when I am by myself. It would not work for me to isolate and have temper tantrums. I just do not do it. I need other people to have temper tantrums. It is the other people that trigger the tantrum. It is the other people that are the objects of my anger. It is the other people who get frightened by my outburst of anger. I do not know how not to have a tantrum. I do not know how to not have them other than to not be around other people. In my work other people are around. I always have a client and I have a staff.

I did not want to have a temper tantrum today at the office. I decided I should go to an AA meeting. AA meetings always calm me down. I am more worried about my temper tantrums than I am about drinking, though I worry about drinking. I want to do everything that gives me the best chance to remember that I am an alcoholic and that I want to stay sober.

I thought by going to an AA meeting I would calm down and I would give the people who work in my office a chance to relax. It would be best for all of us. I went to an AA meeting that I have gone to over the years. It is a women only meeting. I like women only meetings. They feel safer to me. This particular AA meeting is in a church basement. There are no AA slogans on the wall as it is a church and we simply pay to use the room.

The topic of the meeting today was AA slogans in general and the slogan "Easy Does It" in particular. Easy Does It means just what it says- do it easy. There are other AA slogans like "First things first", "think, think, think," "this too shall pass," "let go and let God," but I focused on the "easy does it" slogan when I shared at the meeting. I spoke of the fact that I was stressing at work and that I was getting angry with people at work, that I was really stressing about work, that I was the opposite of easy does it.

As I spoke I wondered could I translate 'easy does it' into my work? I wondered how a jury would feel about me addressing them by saying, "no worries, easy does it." I am not sure that my client would be impressed. Who would want an easy does it lawyer for their lawyer. I do not want to be an easy does it lawyer but I would like to be an easy does it person with those closest to me. And that is precisely what I am not. I am the anti-easy does it person with those closest to me. I do not like that.

When I was doing chemo I was so nice for the most part. Actually I was sick. Sick is nice when I cannot be angry. I was too sick to be angry. That was nice to not get angry. It was nice for me and nice for everyone else. I want to be an easy does it person but not an easy does it lawyer.

I am scared about the surgery. I am scared that the cancer will come back or that they did not get it all. I am worried about work. I am worried for all of the insight I had during chemotherapy that I will not translate all of my insight into action. That scares me more than cancer.

# 29

# THE LUMPECTOMY

I wrote a new will the night before my lumpectomy. I did it to make Woody feel better, more secure. I have a Trust with all of the fancy language. But I am a lawyer and just like any person I can revoke my prior testamentary dispositions whether they be made in a will or a trust and declare a new one without the help of another lawyer or witnesses to validate it so long as the document is dated and written entirely in my own handwriting. Such a will is called a holographic will. It is as valid as a lawyer written document, even when written by a lawyer. Just follow the rules. Write it only in my handwriting, date it and sign it. Those are the rules. I know that. I did it. When I wrote it I realized how incredibly ill prepared I am to die. There are so many things I need to say to people and give to people and be clear about, much less things to do. I wrote the will anyway to make Woody feel better. That just in case any terrible thing happened in surgery, or after surgery or whenever, Woody would get most everything and would be financially okay.

Then I started worrying about how little everything was. I should have been worrying about retirement and savings instead of worrying about whether Oprah Winfrey or Vanessa Redgrave would ever want to meet me and what other people think about me. I have done so much to look good, or what I think other people think looks good. Not all of the time but a lot of the time. I wear expensive clothes. I want to look good. I drive nice cars. I want to look good in my car. I want my car to make me look good. I have had a Volvo 240, a Mercedes 450sl, a Tahoe, a Cadillac Escalade, a Porsche Carrera, and a BMW 325xi which I drive now. That is a lot of money on cars. I should have saved the money.

I should have. What good is the memory of a Porsche going to do if and when I retire? I can show people a photograph of my arena red Porsche and recall its prowess fondly as I eat or don't eat cat food. I won't eat cat food. I do not know what I will do. Who knows if I will make it to retirement? I have always said that I will never retire. I will always work. Why? I think I say that because I think that I have no value unless I am working, unless I am doing something. I am not sure that is what other people think, or what I think other people think. But I think that is what I think. Also by saying that I won't ever retire I do not have to deal with the fact that I have no real meaningful retirement plan. My current plan is just austere spending restrictions and a drastically curtailed lifestyle. That is no plan at all.

I do have a life insurance policy that is renewable for another sixteen years before the company will ask if I had a change in my health. That affirmative answer to the cancer question will put a halt to future life insurance on any affordable level. But if I died this year there is money for Woody as well as another insurance policy that pays off the house and that should be enough. Woody is very frugal and she has some money of her own, so that would be enough. But for me that would not be enough because nothing is ever enough. At least when it comes to money I always seem to want more.

I have had enough of cancer. But maybe cancer is like my distorted thought process and cancer says more is better all the time. I have never really had surgery, not a real surgery, not life threatening surgery. I define real surgery more by exclusion. What I have had is not real surgery. I had my tonsils out when I was 5 years old. That was in England at an army hospital. I spent the night in the hospital. After the surgery they gave me ice cream. I don't remember the surgery. I do remember the ice cream.

One of my tonsils grew back. The one that grew back has never bothered me. I wonder what was wrong with the one that they took if anything. I think in the late 1950's American doctors took out children's tonsils all the time. I was just one of many. I had one tonsil survive and the surviving tonsil is grateful. That surgery was in 1959 or 1960. I did not have another surgery until 1995 and that was arthroscopic knee surgery.

My knees had bothered me for a few years before I had arthroscopic surgery. I had knee surgery to correct the problem or so I thought. In 1995 I did either my left or right knee. Two years later I did my other knee. It was very minor surgery in each case, just some snipping of loose cartilage and cleaning away debris under my kneecap. A few years after the respective surgeries I started going to a chiropractor and figured out that my knee problems were the result of back problems and being out of alignment. I do not regret the knee surgeries. I am not sure that they helped all that much nor did they hurt.

So if anything the surgeries are just a testament to my belief that anyone who had participated in as many athletic activities as I have would require arthroscopic knee surgery. The surgery on each knee was completely in keeping with what I thought people would think and no real examination about what I thought. Maybe I did not think that much. I just knew my knees hurt and I blamed the pain on years of running and power lifting, playing catcher, doing triathlons, falling down, playing field hockey, and especially swimming breast stroke for 15 years doing that whip kick. When things did not get better after the surgery in 1995 I blamed my other knee. I cannot remember which knee came first, nor which came second. I just know I had surgery on each knee.

I had my second arthroscopic knee surgery on Halloween in 1997. I did not think much about it when I went to the hospital on the morning of Halloween. I arrived at the hospital and answered the questions about not having eaten or drank anything and identified what drugs I am allergic to and then the nurse asked me if I wanted something to relax me. I am not sure that she asked, she might have told me. But I knew I was going to get a drug. She brought a Dixie cup filled with some liquid. I drank it. Within seconds literally I felt euphoric and relaxed. I lay on the gurney and wondered partly aloud why I could not have just drank and used in moderation, that I felt so good, better than I ever feel on my own. Within minutes I asked the nurse for another cup of the magic liquid and answered my own question as to why I could not drink and use in moderation. Just like money nothing is ever enough.

Before the nurse could bring me the second cup of the magic liquid as I had convinced her that the first cup had not worked any magic, I passed out. I woke up in the recovery room. No one woke me up. I woke up on my own. I think I woke up before anyone expected me to wake up. I opened my eyes. I saw a scare crow walking and decided I was seeing a woman dressed as a scare crow. Then I saw a woman dressed as a police officer wearing a rubber mask of a pig's face. Then I saw a witch. I wondered about the drug that I had drunk. I wondered if I was tripping. Then my knee pain started and I remembered that I had just had knee surgery and that it was Halloween.

I thought of all of that and then some on the night before my lumpectomy. But this surgery was different. The lumpectomy is not vanity surgery it is life saving surgery. That is heavy. Life saving when I hardly know what my life means to me and that is pretty sad. So I decided not to think about that until after the surgery.

I got to the hospital about 9:30ish a.m. I drove. Woody sat quietly. She brought a bag. She brought the video camera. When we parked the car Woody took out the camera and started filming. I was nervous and was a terrible subject. But Woody tried to engage me. Who knows what the film will show. We had been videoing from the beginning. I have a video of my hair cuts. I have a video of trying wigs on. I reported to the video camera the chemo experience. I have never watched any of the tape. I had the idea to document the experience by videotaping the various steps. The videotaping has worked as a distraction. That is good. Some day the video may even have instructional value, if I can ever watch it.

We got to the same day surgery center on the third floor of St. Luke's and checked in. We got to skip Registration as the same day surgery center takes care of everything. I did not wait long. Woody was with me. Cathy arrived some time after they took me into the pre-op area. They told me to take off my clothes. I was allowed, actually encouraged, to wear my underwear. I knew that. I was worried about that, about what underwear to wear. I wondered if I should wear panties or boxers. I decided to wear both. I did and no one but me knew. I wore my lucky boxers over my lucky panties. I hoped they would be lucky. I gave them my shirt and shorts and bra and shoes. They let me keep my socks on. They gave me a gown and I put it on backwards on purpose so that the opening was in the front instead of the back so that everyone would have easier access to my left breast.

They also gave me a hat. It was a paper hat, like a paper shower cap. It looked stupid but I wore it not just because I was told to wear it but because the paper shower cap looked better then my bald head. I am so tired of being bald. I am more tired of having cancer, but I am still tired of being bald.

I lay on a gurney with the gown on backwards fully protected from whatever unknowns by my panties covered by my boxer shorts and my light blue paper shower cap. I waited. I answered the same questions that I would answer through the course of the day. I said my name. I said my date of birth. I said what drugs I am allergic to and what I was there for. I said, "sentinel node biopsy and left breast lumpectomy." Before my diagnosis I had no real understanding of what either of those procedures entailed. Now I know. I waited some more.

The nurses brought me warm blankets and put them on me and so I felt warm and cozy while I waited. A nurse named Sandy who usually works in the recovery room who had a great Louisiana accent asked me the standard questions. I answered them correctly. My reward was an IV. We discussed which arm and which vein would get the IV. We decided my right arm would be best since my left breast was the object of the surgery. Sandy put a tourniquet around my arm. She tried for my main arm vein, the one that drug addicts use in the movies. It looked good.

Sandy said I had good veins for someone who had just undergone chemotherapy. One of the side effects of chemotherapy is collapsed veins. That shows how bad the chemo drugs are. My veins still look good. But they are tricky and sneaky. Even though my veins plump up and are inviting they squirm to the side to avoid the needle. Most times my veins succeed and the nurse must try again. That is precisely what my right main arm vein did. We picked a new vein in my forearm and I told Sandy about what my veins do, that they are tricky and squirmy. She made appropriate adjustments to her technique and got the IV in my right arm.

I told her even though the IV was giving me saline solution I was still thirsty. She dryly said, "that is because the solution is skipping your mouth". I lay on the gurney awhile longer and explained to all that asked what was to happen to me and where I was to go. A worker came and got me on my gurney and wheeled me to the nuclear medicine department. Woody and Cathy saw me being wheeled away. I called for them to come along. Woody pulled out the video camera. The four of us got into the elevator. When the elevator started and stopped it felt like an amusement park ride. My stomach kind of dropped. Somehow being on a gurney, as well as sitting in a wheelchair, because later when I was transported to another department for another procedure in a wheel chair the same phenomena happened, is like an amusement park ride. The attendant took me to Nuclear Medicine and left me. The nurse there said Woody and Cathy could not come in. She was moderately horrified that I had suggested that the procedure be videotaped.

Woody and Cathy waited in the hallway. They could look into the room because the door has a huge glass window. They looked in and made faces at me. The nurse moved the gurney into another room that had a full wooden door and she shut it. She had witnessed our face making exchanges and consequently moved me. We waited for Dr. Mansfield. Actually she went and got a doctor. Dr. Mansfield was the doctor that she found. He had an English accent. I took that as a good sign since I had lived in England and had my tonsillectomy in England and somewhere my tonsil's remains stayed in England. Somehow it made sense.

I had not taken any drugs before my surgery. I had not smoked pot. I wanted to be present for the experience. I wanted to be able to watch out for myself and I wanted to know what was going on. This was a big deal and I did not want to miss any of it. I was alert when Dr. Mansfield came into the room. We chatted. He told me he was going to inject me with radioactive materials. The injections would be around my nipple and there would be 4, 5, or 6- "it depends" he said. On what he did not elaborate but I think the point was that I should not count. I did not count. Before he started the injections I warned him that I was going to cuss. I told Dr. Mansfield with his very proper British accent that I would most likely say the word "Fuck" and hoped that he would not be offended. I explained that I had gone to Catholic girls schools and had been a very bad girl and simply had never out grown the habit nor found a word more satisfying to say than "fuck".

They positioned my left arm above my head. The nurse told me to squeeze her arm with my left hand. I did. I think I might have hurt her by the power of my squeeze. I squeezed each time Mr. Mansfield injected my nipple. It hurt. It also felt weird to have a needle stuck in my left nipple. During this process I acutely remembered that I had chosen to pierce my left breast nipple. This was worse than that. Each time the doctor stuck the needle in my nipple skin area and injected I squeezed the nurse's hand and said, "Fuck". It all happened very quickly. To any one who could hear I did not shout but I said, "fuckfuckfuckfuckfuck" in rapid fire succession and the procedure was over. Dr. Mansfield laughed and left. The nurse called for someone to wheel me on my gurney back to the pre-op area.

When they opened the door Cathy and Woody were there waiting and we all went down the elevator together. I again commented about how weird it is to be on a gurney in an elevator. They were allowed to wait with me in the pre-op area until they called for me from the breast center. We waited. I stayed calm. When the attendant came for me he brought a wheel chair. I got off the gurney again grateful that I had on panties covered by boxers and sat in the wheel chair. Then I realized that the IV was attached to the gurney. They could not find a pole for the IV so I just carried it. I think Woody got that on the video camera. The four of us rode on the elevator to the breast center. I had to pee. Once we got there it was fun. Dr. Dulcy Wolverton was there and greeted us as did all of the nurses. I was accompanied to the bathroom. Someone had found a pole for my IV. I pushed the pole and walked and was very mobile. I love that I am still mobile. I wanted to appear mobile. Somehow that was important to me.

I went back to the green room. There is a gurney like bed and an ultrasound machine in the room. The room is painted green. There is a window to my left as I lay on the gurney. The shade is drawn somewhat enough to keep out the direct sunlight but not enough to block the view of the tree next to the window. The tree has pretty leaves. This is the room that I lay in when Dulcy first found my cancer. I had the mammograms and then she did the ultrasound on each breast. She knew before she did the ultrasound that there was cancer in my left breast. She knew from looking at the mammograms. I did not exactly know then. I suspected as much, otherwise why would I be getting ultrasounds. That was four months and two weeks ago.

Dulcy again did the ultrasound. The tumor was smaller and had changed shape. Lora came down at some point in the procedure and she and Dulcy talked. Dulcy drew lines on my breast. They talked about how best to do the needle insertions as well as the corresponding surgery. Dulcy made her decisions and then she began by giving me a Novocain injection. I did not watch. I had to keep my left arm above my head. She made a series of injections and put three different needles in my breast that went in and out of my breast at various strategic points. Then all the wires got taped down. I peed again but was not quite as spry as the first time. But still I was agile. The pain had sent me to some other place and I was there but then not there.

I got another mammogram and it was not as bad as I remembered it to be. Maybe there was still Novocain in my breast. My left breast with all its needles was mammogrammed in every possible position. I went to the waiting area and waited. That is when I saw Woody asleep on the couch. Woody was now sick. She had some flu and somehow that made no sense to me. I felt badly for her but at the same time wanted her to magically get better and pay attention to this big thing that was happening to me. I sat in my wheel chair and then was returned to the pre-op area. The same elevator phenomena happened but it no longer seemed so significant. I had stopped talking about it. I was in some zone. I think it is called shock.

When I got back to the pre-op area they put me back on my gurney. I got new warm blankets. The OR nurse was waiting for me as was the anesthesiologist. They asked me the standard questions. The anesthesiologist was a woman. I cannot remember her last name, only her first name, Veronica. She has a French accent. I was impressed that she could speak English well enough to practice medicine here. I think I tried to tell her that I had thought of moving to Norway to live but that I was a lawyer and could not speak Norwegian well enough to work. I am not sure I said that to her but I thought it. I may have said something but by this point I really was not in my body.

Dr. Veronica last name forgotten asked me about my drug allergies. I answered "sulpha drugs". She asked a few more questions and then I remembered that I am allergic to steroids. I do not think of steroids as drugs. I think she explained that I am probably allergic to the preservative meds that are mixed with steroids. She may not have said that, but I think she did. But she told me regardless of the reason I needed to tell people that I am allergic to steroids when asked if I have drug allergies. I will from now on. But hopefully it will never again be important.

Lora came down to the pre-op room. Lora gave me a big hug and reassured me. We were off soon after that. I think there was another elevator ride. I had not been given any drugs but I was out of it now. They pushed the gurney into the operating room. It was cold and stark. I think I tried to talk about courtrooms but am not sure I said anything other than the room was cold. The surgeon determines room temperature. Dr. Veronica says that she wears a polar tech fleece when she works with Lora. I think I said I would too. Somewhere in there I asked if I would get a buzz, or if I could get a buzz. I think Dr. Veronica gave me something that placated me. I do not remember anything after that.

Someone woke me up. It was a nurse. She called my name and I woke up. I had an oxygen mask over my mouth. I lifted my right hand to pull at the mask. The nurse told me not to. I ignored her command. I think she thought I was scratching at my eyes. I do not think I was. I was just trying to get the mask off. The nurse was trying to keep it on. She was telling me it was an oxygen mask. I was trying to tell her that I know what an oxygen mask is and what it is supposed to do and that this mask was not doing it. I am not sure I could talk or was talking. I grabbed at the tubing that ran from the mask and then she finally understood that the mask was not connected to the oxygen tank it was connected to nothing and that is why I wanted the mask off. She fixed it and then my head started to clear.

I think Dr. Veronica came in and checked on me. I asked someone for a shot for pain. My left breast hurt as did my underarm. I got a shot and then another and another. The pain went away. Lora came down and sat with me. I think she brought Woody down. Lora was pleased with the procedure. I think we agreed that we would wait until we saw each other for the post-op appointment to see what the pathology results are. That is fine by me. I hope all the cancer is gone.

When Dulcy was doing the needle procedures I thanked her. There had been some good parts of the cancer. I had met Dulcy. I had met Lora. I had learned about this whole other world. I became a lawyer to help people. They became doctors to help people. They had helped me so much. I think I told them that. I mean it more than anything, that I am grateful beyond belief.

# 30

# THE MORNING AFTER

Woody drove me home from the hospital. Dan, Lora's boyfriend, stood outside the hospital waving to us as we drove off. I thought who is that cute guy waving at us? Woody was sick. I vaguely recall some conversation as to whether Woody was well enough to drive. I do not know how I got to the car. I only remember waving at Dan. Woody went to bed when we got home. Cathy was at the house waiting for us. Cathy gave me chicken noodle soup and crackers. I was still sedated from all of the postoperative painkillers. Whatever they gave me worked throughout the night and my evening was remarkably uneventful.

I was still on drugs when I woke up on the morning after. I also was still nauseous, so I smoked a little pot and the nausea went away. My brother came over around noon. Robert had picked up my friend Illy at the airport. Illy flew in for the weekend from Houston. Illy is B. Ileana Trevino. We have been friends since we were nine years old. Before she was B. Ileana Trevino Illy was B. Ileana Graychowski.

Graychowski was her first husband's name. Before her first marriage Illy was Ileana Vallarino. She lost the Vallarino and added the B. when she married. The initial B. stands for Beatrice, her mother's name. I know Illy as Illy.

Illy has aged remarkably well in that she does not look her age at all. Illy was always good looking and she still is. The years have added an air of sophistication and glamour and the sophistication suits her. So Robert picked up Illy from San Francisco International Airport in his eight year old Midwest Wisconsin Ford Taurus. When Illy arrived at the house the first thing she said to me was, "Where did your brother get that piece of shit car?" Illy said she asked him when she saw him, "Where did you get such a piece of shit car?" She said he said back, "I could eat shit." There was no animus in any of it. It was as if we were all still teenagers.

Illy looked great. I looked like shit. She wore an elegant day outfit. Her hair was tastefully done. Her makeup was impeccably unnoticeable. She carried a big purse. She had become a Texas socialite and yet she is and always will be Illy. If there was any doubt that we really are nothing more than who we were thirty or forty years ago in older bodies that thought was erased on Saturday.

We went to the movies on Saturday after a busy morning. I had a two-hour acupuncture appointment with Dr. Anju Gurnami. Illy accompanied me. Illy walked around Noe Valley and got a manicure and a pedicure and shopped. I whimpered while getting acupuncture because I still hurt from the surgery. I heard Illy talking on the cell phone out front and worried about her having to wait. When I came down from acupuncture she commented that she had been waiting a long time. She had and so what. We laughed.

All of the movies we really wanted to see were exclusive engagement movies at theaters not so close. So we settled on The Brave One with

Jody Foster. We headed towards one theater only to learn that the show time had been changed from what the newspaper reported. We would either be very late or have to wait a really long time. Neither choice was acceptable so we headed to another theater. This other theater is an old theater. Only old people go there not because it is old, but because the theater is all on one floor. It is easy for old people to get in and out of the theater as well as within the theater. We bought our tickets and went in. The bathroom was messy and gross and inevitably as Illy complained about how gross the bathroom was she pushed open a stall door to see a toilet filled with every bodily fluid possible. Illy screamed, "this place is disgusting." She was right it was. I was still pretty weak from surgery and did not really care.

I have spent weeks on end in the Himalayas with no plumbing and only pit toilets. I have been in third world countries where the disgusting theater bathroom would be pristine. Years ago in the brand new Ulan Bataar Airport in Mongolia they had built beautiful bathrooms. I had to use one. I went in and was very impressed by the brand new airport because the old one had been a dump. This was one of the first days since the new airport had opened. I went into a stall and peed. I flushed the toilet and it did not flush. I tried again and it did not flush. I gave up and went to a sink to wash my hands. Neither faucet worked- no cold water nor any hot water. I tried another sink with the same results. I tried every sink. I returned to the various toilet stalls and tried to flush the various toilets and none flushed. Apparently no one had connected the water to the bathroom. Suffice to say in a few days the beautiful bathroom was a mess because no one connected the water. The movie theater bathroom did not bother me.

We went to the designated theater. It was huge and empty as we were early. We picked what we thought would be good seats and sat down. Within a minute a middle- aged man sat down behind us and started breathing hard. We got up and moved to other seats in a different section to get away from the hard breathing pervert. The theater was still very empty. The house lights were up. Commercials were playing on the screen. There were commercials for energy drinks, plus Sprite and Diet Coke. There were commercials to rent the theater. There were commercials for television shows. Illy and I watched the commercials and did not chat much. The truth was at that point I did not feel well enough to talk.

Sometime during the commercials and a few minutes before the scheduled show time a woman about our age but somehow older left her seat a row or two in front of ours and walked towards us. Her seat was in the center. Our seats were aisle seats. The rows were long 30 plus seats across. She walked over about 15 seats and addressed us. I smiled at her expecting a warm exchange. Instead she said, "My friend and I came to the movies to watch the movie and we do not appreciate listening to you two and your nonstop talking."

I was incredulous for several reasons. First of all we were barely talking. Second of all the show had not started. The house lights were up and they were playing commercials. I replied to her complaint, "We were not talking very much but now we will." That made her more angry. Illy tried to reason with her by pointing out the show had not started and the house lights were on and commercials were being played and other people were talking.

The woman did not respond. She walked back to her seat and sat down. Illy and I looked at each other and laughed. The complainant turned to us and said in a voice loud enough for anyone who wanted to listen to hear: "You two are sick." That made me laugh even harder. I said, "You are right I have cancer." She should have noticed when she came over to scold us. I barely have any eyebrows left and was wearing a bandana to hide my bald head. I looked like someone who was doing or had just done chemotherapy. The complaining lady retorted, "We all have something."

That reply was true. We all do have something but in that instance no something seemed as bad as cancer. She looked pretty good. She had her hair, her real hair and not a wig. She could walk without assistance. She could talk and hear and engage in some thought process, albeit clearly limited. She felt sure enough of herself to come over and chastise us during commercials with the house lights on. We do all have something. But I decided when I heard her say that, that whatever her something was, it was not as bad as my something and I wanted to hurt her feelings. I had just done 16 weeks of chemotherapy, lost my hair, thrown up, been poked, stuck, radiated, infused, scared, frightened, confused and just had surgery and was still worried about the pathology report. I could not ignore "We all have something". I had to say something back to her.

I said back to her, "Yea, well you are stupid." I paused. Stupid was not enough. I did not want to cuss at her because that could get me in trouble, like getting us kicked out of the movie theater. But calling her stupid was not enough. So I told her, "and you are ugly". Then I looked at Illy. We laughed and laughed and laughed. I knew what I had just said was stupid. Illy told me that what I said was "more lame than stupid." That is how sick I was, that the best that I came up with is that the complainant was stupid and ugly. We tried to be quiet. We noticed that all the rest of the theater patrons were talking while we quietly laughed. The complainant and her friend just sat there. They were neither laughing nor talking. After a few minutes of strained silence between the complainant and us the lights went down and the real coming attractions started. We started laughing again.

I was not laughing to be rude or mean. By that point I was laughing because the whole thing was so stupid that it was funny. Both Illy and I thought we were going to have a pleasant encounter and instead we were reprimanded. It was like being in grade school.

The movie was gruesome enough from the start that we stopped laughing. We left the theater after the movie was over but before the house lights came up to avoid any further confrontation with the complainant. We skipped the bathroom because it really was gross.

The whole ridiculous and juvenile experience made me feel good. Laughing with Illy made me feel good. Talking with her and knowing that we have so much history in common was very reassuring. Illy told the movie story to everyone she called- Michael her husband and all her children. They all knew that I was not feeling well because they each expected much better of me than " You are stupid and ugly" That was the best that I had that day which was not very good.

The weekend flew by which is what I wanted it to do. I wanted time to go by quickly to Thursday when I would meet with Lora and go over the pathology report. Then I would know whether the cancer was gone.

# 31

# LORA CALLED ON TUESDAY

I went to the office on Monday and worked. I tried not to lose my
temper with anyone including myself. I went to an AA meeting
at lunch and relaxed there. I had lunch at my mother's and visited
with her. My brother, Robert was at my office working. Robert was a
football coach for some 20 plus years and then on my encouragement
went to law school. He graduated this May and took the bar exam in
July. He started working for me a few weeks ago. I tried not to yell
at Robert or Kelton, my associate that made the mistake at Avenal
State Prison, or anyone and went to the meeting. For the most part I
succeeded. But I was tired. I was worried about my pathology results.
I hoped that there was no cancer in my lymph nodes. I hoped that
there was no cancer left in the tumor. I hoped that the margins
were acceptable, meaning that there was enough cancer free tissue
surrounding the cancerous tumor such that a further surgery would
not be necessary to remove any remaining cancer.

In the days since my surgery I have thought of Lora Burke my breast surgeon with such affection and admiration and gratitude. I look at my breast and am so grateful that lefty is still with me and that lefty looks pretty good. Lefty is with me because of Dr. Michelle Bourgault. I saw Michelle because Susan Travers, my hair stylist, the one I spent all the money on, introduced me to Michelle one afternoon when Michelle was just leaving after Susan had done her hair and I was just arriving for Susan to do my hair. Now I have no hair. Susan no longer does hair having altered her lifestyle by learning to sail, buying a sail boat and then sailing to Tahiti. And Michelle gently reminds me that I need to come in for a gynecological checkup.

Michelle sent me to Dr. Dulcy Wolverton who read my mammogram and did the ultrasounds, all of them, and put the needles in my breast that helped Dr. Lora Burke to perform the lumpectomy. I looked at my breast and there is not much of a scar and the bruising although very colorful, kind of like autumn leaves, is dissipating. The incision under my underarm is remarkably small and not very swollen. Clearly Lora did a great job. But still I worried. I do not want anymore cancer. As much as I enjoy seeing Lora I would prefer not to have her perform another surgery. So I worried. I had not worried too much Friday because I was still semi-euphoric from the anesthesia and morphine. Illy was here over the weekend so that was Illy time and I worried more that she thought that I looked bad, which I did, than about pathology results. Monday I was grumpy. I was still grumpy on Tuesday.

I was at the office at lunch. I had bought miso soup, steamed vegetables and rice. I had an acupuncture appointment with Dr. Anju Gurnami at 2 p.m. Anju told me to eat my lunch before the appointment. I do what Anju tells me to do. I wanted to eat a good lunch in case Anju asked me what I ate for lunch. I wanted to impress her. But I was tired and a little mopey because I knew that I had another two days until I would see Lora and she would tell me my pathology results. I had thought about calling her or emailing her but we had made a deal not to talk until Thursday at 10 a.m. at her office for my post surgery appointment. I sat at my desk eating steamed vegetables and working. I was anxious. I got up to get a file and my cell phone rang.

My cell phone does not ring. My cell phone plays a song, a hip- hop song when the phone can read the name or the numbers of the caller. It is a catchy tune. It makes me want to hip- hop dance. On one of my bad chemo days when I was very sick from adriomyacin/cytoxin around the time that I quit taking the prescribed antinausea drugs that made me homicidal or suicidal and switched to smoking pot I changed my cell phone ring tone. I had friends over at the house. We were all sitting around the table. I was being sick. My cell phone rang, meaning that the hip- hop song played. I got up to answer the phone and started dancing hip- hop style. We all laughed. We all had cell phones. Another cell phone rang meaning that it played some song and as it played its ring tone I started dancing. I stopped when my friend answered her phone. And so it went for the rest of the afternoon. Each time a phone rang we all got up and danced until the phone was answered and when the phone was answered we each stopped dancing. It made for a fun game, some weird play on musical chairs. Any time a cell phone goes off in any place everyone in hearing distance should have to get up and dance until the call is answered. It is a fun game.

That tired Tuesday in my office I did not dance to the song as my phone played. I was tired. I just answered the phone with not a lot of life. I said hello without very much enthusiasm. The voice on the other phone said, "Hi Paula, this is Lora." I immediately wanted a do over. If I knew it was Lora calling I would have answered with a big hello. I told her so and changed my attitude and my voice to convey how happy I was to hear her voice.

Lora said, "Do you want the good news or the really good news first?" Then I knew she was calling with good news. I am not sure I even answered her question before she told me the news that my margins were good that there were only 51 cancer cells in what by all accounts was a very dead cancerous tumor. Clearly the chemotherapy had killed the tumor. Lora told me that there was no cancer in my lymph nodes. I was thrilled. So was Lora. We talked and talked and talked. My heart was absolutely filled with love for Lora. It always is, really. I was and am so happy that Lora did not have to tell me bad news. I am equally happy that I did not have to hear any more bad news from anyone.

Somewhere during the conversation I asked Lora why she was calling me; that I thought we had a deal that we would find out the results together. Lora explained that is her little trick. I understand the trick. It makes sense to me, that she does not want anyone to hear bad news over the phone. I am glad that Lora called. I would have been fine to wait until Thursday because I would do whatever Lora wanted and I wanted to respect her protocol. For all that she has done for me I figured it was the least that I could do. That is my news, good news and more good news.

I thanked Lora. In fact I thanked her and thanked her and thanked her again. I like thanking her. Then I called Woody and told her. Woody's first question after exclaiming how great was whether or not I still had to do radiation. That seems like a fair and valid question. When I saw Anju, the acupuncturist, she asked me the same question. As my feet and legs still tingle a bit from the Taxol I wondered if radiating a breast that now has no cancer left because of the chemotherapy is like dropping more bombs on Hiroshima.

I have more decisions to make. I believe that I have made good ones thus far. I want to keep making good decisions. I have had good advice regarding the decisions I have made. I have followed the advice of my doctors, except when I have not.

But if I am free of cancer why would I want more treatment to kill cancer that is not there. With respect to estrogen inhibitors why don't doctors give everyone estrogen inhibitors so that they do not get estrogen driven tumors. I think I like my estrogen, what little there is in me. I am prone to depression. If I have no estrogen I am afraid that I will get depressed. There is a connection between estrogen loss and depression. The truth is I do not want cancer again. This is one of those areas that potentially the solutions may create problems. I am wondering if I even have a problem any more since I do not have any cancer in me.

# 32

# WHY DID I GET CANCER

I have started reading medical books and self help books about breast cancer. I think it is fair question. Why did I get breast cancer? I have no family history of cancer. I have a lot of the other criteria. I worry. I do not sleep enough. I work too much. I eat too much red meat and not enough raw vegetables. I do not drink now but I did. I drank for almost 20 years from 12ish to 31. I drank a lot. I smoked cigarettes from that same age and then a few more years. I did every drug available. I sniffed Freon. I snorted cocaine, took pills, smoked opium and heroin, dropped acid, and ate mushrooms. There really is nothing that I have not done except shoot drugs, only because I am afraid of needles.

I have been sober for some 21 years. I thought I had purged myself of the effects of my bad behavior by clean living and exercise. Apparently not. I have spent as much money on therapy as I have on cars over the course of the last 21 years just to have a feeling that is appropriate to an event at the time of the event that gives rise to the feeling. That has cost me thousands of dollars and hours and days over twenty years.

I did not know about feelings. I knew anger. But there are more feelings than anger, but that is the only one I knew how to experience. I always knew there were other feelings I just did not know the experience of them. I had to learn the feelings. I was 44 years old when I learned about feelings. I lived 44 years without ever really experiencing sadness as sadness. When I felt sad I got angry. When I felt lonely I got angry. When I felt pain I got angry. When I was afraid I got angry. When I felt guilt I got angry. When I felt shame I got angry. I rarely felt joy or happiness. I just tried to keep busy so that I would not feel anything.

At some point I realized that by getting angry I was blaming other people for whatever it was that I was feeling and somehow that did not seem right. I turned a great deal of the anger inward and eventually I became depressed and I still did not really understand any of it. When I was so depressed that I truly wished myself dead I went to a treatment program called the Meadows in Wickenburg Arizona. I went because I was depressed. I was more afraid that I would not kill myself but that I would drink. I did not want to drink so much that I went to a program. It was at the Meadows that I learned about feelings and identifying them and experiencing them.

I worked so hard there. I relived my most painful emotional experiences and experienced the feelings that I should have had at the time of the experience. I had carried so much baggage in the form of unresolved conflict about painful experiences because I had not experienced the true feeling that went with the experience. I did that for all of my worst traumas. I did that for being raped, for being molested, for feeling helpless and frightened. The irony is that when I had the feeling I was freed of the experience. I had spent 44 years afraid to have a feeling mistakenly believing that by keeping feelings at bay I was in control. Precisely the opposite is true.

I wonder if I have cancer because I kept my feelings bottled up inside for 44 years. I was not some robot for 44 years. I was a worker and did lots of good work. I have helped many, many people. I have always been kind and generous. Arguably I am codependent. I am codependent. I have joked that the gift of my alcoholism is that when drinking I could not meddle in other peoples business with the gusto that I could with each successive year of sobriety.

It has taken me so long to understand that sometimes giving things or doing things for others is not the best way to help. Sometimes not helping is the best way to help. There is a very complicated relationship between my thoughts and my feelings and my actions. I did not understand the interrelationship until recently. Instead I blamed a lot of other people for everything. That makes me laugh now. There is of course plenty of appropriate times to assign culpability to another. But there is never a time to blame another for what I feel. That is my responsibility. That is my blessing. And that is the irony of life, of my life, of everyone's life. I ran from me and I was the one running. Everywhere I go it is me that I am taking with me as I run. There is no getting away from me by me no matter how hard I have tried. How silly for me to have spent so much of my life trying to do the impossible. Perhaps that is why I got cancer. Perhaps that is why I will not get cancer again because I no longer try to do the impossible. After all these years I no longer suffer from the incessant criticism my mind levels against me.

There is no drug, no liquor, no pill, no work, no thrill, no adventure, no person that can keep me from me unless I let it. I do not think I want that to happen ever again. My whole life has been about putting myself back together, for all of me to be at the same place at the same time and for me to be at peace with myself and not use people, places, and things as an excuse for my failure to be comfortable and accept who I am. That is what having cancer has taught me. I would have preferred not to have gotten cancer. I would have preferred to know all that I know without difficult lessons. I believe as long as the cancer does not come back that I got the better end of the deal. I have learned far more and know far more than the difficulty of the lessons. I think that is true for all of us. It has just taken me a very long time to understand that I no longer have so much difficulty with being me. Cancer was a small price to pay for my lesson. I can say that only because I believe I no longer have cancer.

I got cancer to learn a lesson, many lessons. One of the most important lessons I have learned is that I do not want to have to get cancer in order to learn more lessons. I may be wrong about why I got cancer. I may just have been one of the random people who get cancer. There may be nothing philosophical in the getting. It may just be bad luck and nothing more. And it may just be good luck in getting rid of it and nothing less.

# 33

# THE DIFFICULTY WITH BEING ME (Even at Sanoviv)

October 15, 2007

I am at another treatment program. This one is called Sanoviv. It is in Rosorita Mexico, which means so am I. Sanoviv is a health institute. I am going to have my cells studied while I eat organic food and wear organic cotton clothing. I am doing this to try to find out why I got breast cancer and perhaps more importantly what I can do so that I never again get another cancer.

I think I know the answer. I think I am emotionally short- circuited. I think I always have been. It has just taken this long for the short-circuiting to hit my body. Before, I engaged in various behaviors that they themselves were so pathological, I never really had time to get cancer.

My alcoholism was pathological. Then I got sober but did not really deal with the root cause of my alcoholism. My alcoholism is more than an allergy to alcohol. My alcoholism is but one of the many manifestations of my fundamental problem.

I suffer from D.W.B.M. The diagnosis is not in any D.S.M. book. The D.S.M. is the diagnostic manual for psychological disorders. For example P.T.S.D. is in the D.S.M. as a recognizable diagnosable disorder. P.T.S.D. is post traumatic stress disorder. I have P.T.S.D. I have alcoholism. But they both are just manifestations of D.W.B.M. which is not in the D.S.M.

I learned the term from my friend Lisa Weindorf. Lisa did not say D.W.B.M. She did say that at times she has difficulty with being herself or words to that effect. I just put initials to the term. And that is what I have D.W.B.M.- difficulty with being me.

My D.W.B.M. has manifested as alcoholism, workaholism, depression, anxiety, and ultimately cancer. I am not sure that is true. The statement implies that I caused my cancer. I am not sure that is true. I am also not sure that it is not. I don't know.

So I have come to Sanoviv to figure that out. Somewhere in the inquiry is yet again another opportunity for me to address the fact of my life that I still have so much difficulty with being comfortable with being me. I have confronted my D.W.B.M. over and over. Each time something happens or I do something and I am back to dealing with my D.W.B.M. I have difficulty with being me now because I had cancer. But I think I got cancer because I have so much difficulty being me.

So far at Sanoviv I don't start out so much as me. I am the only bald woman here. Most of the people look healthy. I look healthy now just bald. They give you clothes here, cotton clothes. Everyone must dress in the cotton clothes provided. There are grey cotton shorts, or sweats and various styles of t-shirts and sweatshirts and organic socks. Everyone must wear sandals. So we all dress alike with some varieties of mix and match. But there is no mistaking that we are essentially in organic cotton uniforms.

I joked we look like cult members. We do. I joked before coming here that I will be fine unless they ask us all to drink the Kool Aid. No need to worry about that as there is no Kool Aid here.

There is no sugar here.

# 34

# THAT WHICH I AM LOOKING FOR IS THAT WHICH IS LOOKING

Mornings at Sanoviv begin with meditation. Actually this morning began with the collection of urine, saliva, and stool samples, not at the same time, nor with the same containers, nor in public. In the privacy of my room, in the privacy of my beautiful all marble bathroom I collected the various samples. I hated it. Even alone I hated it, not the saliva. It is easy to spit in a plastic cup. But for me and most women it is tricky to pee in a plastic cup. As for the stool AKA shit I think it is awkward for anyone, man or woman to defecate onto a cardboard tray and scoop the stool, using the wooden tongue depressor supplied in the collection kit into the plastic container. But I did it.

The stress of shitting into a cardboard tray has made me constipated. That worries me that they will know I have issues because I have issues about shitting onto a cardboard tray. I did all that before our first activity of morning meditation.

I have meditated over the years. I first consciously learned about mediation at the Betty Ford Center. At the Betty Ford Center when being given initial instruction about mediation I remembered I had received similar instruction years earlier. It was my junior year in high school while attending Georgetown Visitation College Preparatory School for Young Ladies. Visitation is the oldest Catholic girl's school in the original 13 colonies. Apparently there is a Catholic girl's school located in Louisiana that was founded some years before Georgetown Visitation. Even though I attended Visitation it was not until I was editing this that I actually learned the story of Visitation's founding.

For years I have been saying that I went to high school at Georgetown Visitation College Preparatory School for Young Ladies. For years I have been saying that Visitation is the oldest school in the United States. For years I have been telling people that Georgetown Visitation was founded by an extraordinary woman who had been widowed after having many children. In my story the widow sought to join various religious orders but was rejected because she had been married. After numerous rejections she did the only thing she could do. She founded her own order called the Sisters of the Visitation and opened Georgetown Visitation in 1799. I could not remember the founder's name. So I called my old high school. The receptionist answered and I asked the name of the school's founder. The receptionist did not know. I asked to be transferred to someone who might be able to give me the requested information. I waited.

A voice on the other end answered, "Sister Mary Berchmans." Sister Mary Berchmans was the headmistress of Georgetown Visitation when I was in high school. Her first year as Headmistress was my freshman year. We had quite a stormy few years. Sr. Berchmans expelled me and later allowed me to return and ultimately graduate. From Sister Berchmans I learned that I had most of the story wrong.

The Visitation Order was founded in 1610 by Jane Frances de Chantel in Annecy France with Francis de Sales, both of whom later were canonized and consequently are called Saints. So the Visitation Order was founded by a woman, but the Order was founded in France, not America and some 160 years earlier than what I had believed.

The school Georgetown Visitation was founded by three women who took over an old convent that had been abandoned by some French nuns of the Poor Clares Order.

The three women were not nuns. They were helping Bishop Leonard Neal who had been assigned to go to Georgetown to work on Georgetown University. The three women took over the abandoned convent and began to run a girls school. In the convent they found the Constitution of the Visitation Order. They read it. They liked it. So they decided the school would be part of the Visitation Order. That was a good choice.

The Visitation Order back then was a slightly radical Order in both its inception and its philosophy. Unlike other convents of the day Visitation practiced Salesian Spirituality as opposed to the Austere, harsh traditional "spirituality" of the day. In other words Visitation nuns did not have to self- flagellate and starve. Sister Berchmans told me, "Let your feet be well shod but your heart stripped bare." All these new facts, correct facts, have thrown me especially since I like my old story better. Regardless of how Visitation came to be, it remains true that at my junior year retreat I learned about meditating.

My junior year at Visitation was 1971. I was living at the boarding school part by choice and part by order. I had gotten into more trouble than just about anyone in the school in my sophomore year. My choice after attending a public high school for two days and then dropping out was either stay expelled or live at the boarding school. I chose to live at the boarding school. In the spring the junior class took a class retreat at a Franciscan Retreat Center. One of the classes was about meditation. I remember sitting quietly and knowing that if only I would not drink alcohol I would not have so many problems.

But I forgot what I knew in my heart within a few weeks. I do not remember when I forgot what I knew in my heart, or what caused me to forget. I have heard that the "ism" of alcoholism stands for "incredible short memory". I forgot. I drank a drink and then another again and again until some 15 years later I wound up at Betty Ford's at meditation class and remembered what I had forgotten - that alcohol is a problem for me.

I know that alcohol consumption by me is but a symptom of my problem. It is a symptom of D.W.B.M. The reality is though when I was drinking I was causing so many problems that no one including me saw past the problems. For example I got drunk and drove a car and wrecked it. Everyone including me dealt only with the wrecked car and how to solve that problem. The wrecked car completely distracted everyone from the real problem which was me.

A person is composed of mind, body, spirit and emotion. I now believe that is true. I used to believe that a person was just mind and body and that the emotional part was silly and the spiritual part was some sort of institutional brainwashing for control over the individual and monetary gain for some religious institution. I have since decided that the concepts are not mutually exclusive.

I believe now that the emotional part of me is very rich and compelling. I believe that the spiritual part is all that as well and then some. So I went to mandatory morning mediation with a somewhat open mind. I was reminded of all that I know. I was reminded that I am mind, body, spirit and emotions. I believe that the four of us may be a little out of alignment. I believe we are one breast cancer tumor out of alignment.

All things considered that is not so bad. That I am here at all is a miracle. So I am here at Sanoviv and did a guided mediation. The leader said the words that reminded me that I went to Betty Ford's and received mediation instruction which reminded me I had received meditation instruction at age 17 which reminded me that at age 17 I knew drinking was causing me problems and was no solution. Yet I kept drinking. I stopped at Betty Ford's. But I ignored what I knew to be true for fourteen years. If I ignore what I know to be true I know that my spiritual part wants more room in my life. The spiritual part is what I long for and what I seek. I know I need look no farther than myself.

I know that which I am looking for is that part of me that looks.

That part of me that when I meditate is quiet is what I seek and occasionally find and most consistently ignore. It is that little voice in my head or my heart that experientially says, "Look out or watch out" and loves. I have to figure out how to elevate my spiritual life from a thought to an experience that is part of my daily life.

# 35

# CHEMOTHERAPY CAUSES VAGINAL ATROPHY

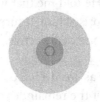

I have an atrophied vagina, or maybe it is my uterus, or maybe my cervix. It is hard to think about spirituality when I have just failed my pelvic exam. Failing the exam are my words not the Doctor's. I had my Sanoviv pelvic exam today at 7:30 A.M. That is the earliest my pelvis has ever been examined by a doctor. As to non health care professionals, that is another story and outside the scope of this discourse for now.

Yesterday I met my doctor as I am at Sanoviv for the Complete Health Assessment. The Complete Health Assessment is a diagnostic regimen, like a super physical. I want a complete health assessment to see how much damage I did to myself from the chemotherapy. The Doctor, Dr. Isaac Meza, took a long medical history from me ranging from operations and hospitalizations and family history. Somewhere in there he asked me the number of sexual partners I have had. Earlier in the medical history he had asked my marital status and I told him I am not married, and that I am a lesbian and that I am in a good, stable long- term relationship. I could answer the questions about hospitalizations and operations but the sexual partner question surprised me. I think my doctor was surprised when I could not answer.

When Dr. Meza asked, "How many sexual partners have you had?" or words to the effect, I said I had to count. I counted in my head. I blurted out "over 20". I continued blurting, "There were more men than women, more than ten men" I sounded like the Dustin Hoffman character in Rain Man and again said, "More than ten men." The doctor stopped me. He told me that was enough information. I think "more than 20" surprised him. It surprised me. But the number conveyed that I have been sexually active.

So I stopped speaking as he directed, but continued thinking intermittently throughout the remainder of the interview, and then the rest of the day about the number of sexual partners. The more I thought the longer the list became of both men and women. The final tally last night was over 30 evenly divided between men and women. I remembered all the women's names but not the men and I never knew the name of the man who raped me. I decided I would not tell the doctor my revised count or that there was virtual equilibrium in the sexes. I do not think that was important to him. It is not particularly important to me except no doctor has ever asked me that question before. If it is important enough for a doctor to ask it is important for me to know.

Now I know.

I was his first appointment of the day. I wondered as I undressed if he thought about my sexual history, "more than ten men". I doubt he was expecting to start his day with an atrophied vagina, especially not one that belonged to a promiscuous lesbian. But so it was. I did not know my vagina had atrophied. I knew I had not had sex since I started chemotherapy. I nevertheless thought that I was good to go.

I lay on the table and put my feet in the stirrups and my knees framed my face, practically. I had not had a pelvic exam in at least a year. The nurse was there she smiled at me. Dr. Meza readied the speculum and told me to relax and take a deep breath. I did take a deep breath but I did not relax. I took deep breath after deep breath while Dr. Meza tried to insert the speculum in my vagina with virtually no success. I kept taking deep breaths until Dr. Meza told me to stop because he thought I was going to pass out. I did stop just in time because I felt as if I was going to pass out. I said, "I bet you didn't think this was going to happen." Then I apologized, that I had no idea what was wrong with me. Dr. Meza explained that my vagina had atrophied, and that was a consequence of chemotherapy. He told me not to worry. He told me that I would get better. I asked how does one un-atrophy a vagina. He smiled. If he heard me at all he did not reply, perhaps thinking it was a rhetorical question. He again reassured me and said I would get better. Even though the doctor told me not to worry, I did worry.

I worried so much I skipped breakfast and wheat grass juice. I worried so much I immediately came back to my room, lay on the bed and worried about my shrunken uterus and recessed cervix. The doctor was right my uterus had shrunk and my cervix had recessed. Apparently the chemo did affect my uterus and I am left with a soft cervix recessed back. I wondered what to do. I do not want an atrophied vagina. The doctor said, "we will try again", referencing another attempt at a pap smear. So I have a few days to un-atrophy. But sex and how to get back into sex shape was the farthest thing from my mind. I just do not want to flunk another pelvic exam. So I decided I simply would not have another pelvic exam, ever.

Later in the day I met with Dr. Meza to review my test results and to hear his recommendations. I was still worried about the pelvic exam, my failed pelvic exam. When we met my doctor again told me not to worry, that what happened was a consequence of the chemo. I wondered how much of me had atrophied from chemo. Dr. Meza assured me that I was in remarkably good shape in spite of the chemo.

Dr. Isaac Meza is great. I have been blessed with great doctors all the way through this process. Dr. Isaac later went over all my tests with me. I am in good shape. He recommended staying on Herceptin. He recommended doing radiation. He also recommended alternative treatments and switching from the detox program to the medical program while at Sanoviv. That meant undergoing more medical procedures, including chelation, hyperbaric chamber oxygen treatments, and body baking procedures.

At first I balked. I thought there had to be some other way. I do not think there is. I think this is the way to go. I think I should get as much as I can. So I switched to the medical program and got treatments in the hyperbaric chamber and special heat treatments and chelation.

But I still am worried about my atrophied vagina and intend to call Michelle my gynecologist. I am confident Michelle can find my cervix. Enough about that. Me and my vagina will heal.

# 36

# CHECKING MY TEETH

As part of the Compete Health Assessment each guest, that is what people are called at Sanoviv, not patients, but guests, is examined by a dentist. I hate the dentist. I filled out a dental questionnaire so the dentist would know that I did not want to be examined. But I let him. He did the exam. It was not bad because he did not play with my gums because they are still recovering from chemotherapy. Chemotherapy hurts gums and it takes time for them to heal. Luckily they are still in the healing process and consequently could not safely be examined. I am more forgiving as to my gums than I am as to my vagina.

On the third day my diet changed from organic, fat free, wheat free, dairy free, meat free, seafood free, sugar free, pepper free, salt free organic food to organic liquids. Everything came in a bowl. The first bowl tasted awesome, though I cannot remember what it tasted like.

But with each meal my satisfaction has diminished. This says a lot more about me than it does about the food.

On the third meal of liquid food breakfast a fellow guest offered me a piece of her hemp granola. I wanted something crunchy. I wanted something sweet. The hemp granola looked to be both. I took a handful. It was only crunchy. One out of two was enough for me to take a second handful.

I crunched covertly. I should have declined the hemp granola. But it wasn't just that I was hungry I was also curious. I had no idea there was such a thing as hemp granola. I ate the second handful then went to my room. I had to brush my teeth to get rid of the evidence, not that anyone was looking. Brushing was not enough. I had to see the dentist later for my follow up. Flossing was called for to hide any trace of my hemp granola.

I flossed. Almost immediately the floss hit a piece of granola or some sharp part of what I later learned is tooth 13. The floss stuck. I pulled on the floss. Tooth 13 broke. Not all of it, just a part of it. Just enough for my tongue to spend the entire rest of the day playing with broken tooth 13.

There is a lobby in the main building where everyone waits to be called for treatments. I waited in the lobby for my 'treatment' using my poor irritated tongue to continue checking to see if tooth 13 was still broken. Each time my tongue checked tooth 13 was broken. It stayed that way. My treatment person arrived.

My treatment was a colonic. I have never had a colonic before. Basically a colonic treatment person sticks a tube in one's rectum that flushes the large intestine with water. The water stays in the intestine until the bowels start moving and expel the water with fecal material. There's a machine that does the pumping. I don't really understand how it works. Water goes in and feces and water come out through another tube. The tubes are clear so that both the subject and the therapist can see the expelling waste.

I sweated. It was so stressful that my tongue forgot to check about my broken tooth. I failed miserably in colonic therapy. My therapist seemed disappointed in my failure to excrete much waste. Somehow the tube disengaged. That was my fault as well. The therapist stuck the tube in my rectum again and tried to reassure me.

Water went in and in. This seemed to please her. At some point I said I needed to use the bathroom. I disengaged and went into the privacy of a bathroom. I just am not capable of watching expelled fecal material with anyone. In the privacy of the toilet all that came in came out. The coming out process continued for longer than the going in process.

Another guest was arriving on the hour so I eventually had to get out of there. I made it to my room, only to experience more of the same. I can hardly talk about the experience much less think that one could talk calmly with another person about the shit coming out of their body.

People do that. The colonics lecturer talked all about the way she examines her fecal material. She is absolutely fascinated by not just her own fecal material but anyone's, actually everyone's fecal material. She has a colonics practice. As it turns out many of the guests here are quite familiar with colonics and many swear by the therapy.

I am not in that group and actually am not sure that it is such a good idea. I want things to move out not in and out. Before truly recovering from the colonic I was summoned to the dentist for my follow up. The dentist showed me my x-rays and told me which teeth needed work. I told him about my broken tooth and showed him.

He told me that the broken tooth was tooth 13 and it was dead already. Tooth 13 had a root canal about three years ago. Root canals are controversial he explained. Cutting the root essentially leaves a dead tooth in the mouth. His recommendation is pulling the tooth so that the dead tooth is removed from the mouth.

I inquired what was to go in the space of the missing dead tooth. He suggested a cap. I wondered to myself if my gums were not healthy enough to withstand the trauma of extracting tooth 13. I am sure my still not recovered gums as well as tooth 12 and tooth 14 would miss 13. The rest of me did not want to loose 13. Even my left breast said she was saved and expressed her desire that 13 stay with us.

I was far less concerned about 13 regardless of his recommendations. 13 was and is staying. I was far more concerned with the three mercury amalgam fillings in my mouth. I do not recall when they were put there. It had to have been either in my teens or in my late thirties. I am not sure. I know those time periods are fairly accurate not that I remember cavities, because I don't. But I do remember for the years that I lived on my own and was still drinking I did not go to the dentist, except one time and that was to fix a broken tooth. That may have been the first time I broke 13.

The second time I broke 13 I was in Nepal. It was March 1999. I was eating popcorn. I was on my way up. I had walked to Jorsele for four days to get to the point where I would take the just popped popcorn from a farmer to take a bite and break tooth 13. I was still a day's walk from meeting Chombi. There was nothing to do but eat another piece of popcorn and keep on walking.

When I got back to the States some 25 days later I called my dentist. He tried to fix it. But eventually number 13 died. I paid a different dentist to do the root canal because I blamed the first dentist and not the popcorn for killing 13. I still don't really believe 13 is dead. I love 13 in all her root canalled brokenness.

I just do not understand why any of the dentists that I have seen over the past 15 years or so failed to talk to me about my three mercury amalgam fillings. The dentist who just recommended extraction of tooth 13 had plentiful information about the dangers of mercury amalgam fillings and recommended they be replaced.

I cannot deal with dental work right now. But I can express absolute shock that any dentist ever put mercury in anyone's mouth for any purpose. Ever since I was very young some 45 years ago I knew mercury was toxic. I was very young some 45 years ago. Those fillings are a lot younger than 45 years.

I had no idea anyone put mercury anything in my teeth. I did some additional checking. In 1988 the Environmental Protection Agency declared scrap dental amalgam to be hazardous waste. There is hazardous waste material in 3 of my teeth. The amalgam fillings are silver in color and I vaguely remember them being called silver fillings. Amalgams are not just silver. Only 35% of the amalgam is silver. The other components are approximately 9% tin, 6% copper, and a trace of zinc. The other remaining 50% is mercury.

Mercury is one of the worst toxic substances known to man. Who on earth would use it to make a tooth filling. Mercury is toxic. Mercury toxicity impairs kidney function, contributes to cardiovascular disease, neuropsychological dysfunction, fatigue, and insomnia. Mercury causes lots of problems. The list goes on and on. The filling releases mercury vapors. Every day since whenever they were put in my mouth I have been breathing mercury vapors. And every day my immune system has had to fight off the vapors from impairing the other cells within me.

It seems that for many, many years the American Dental Association asserted that the mercury amalgam was a tightly bound chemical complex that would not permit any leakage or release of mercury. There were studies proving them wrong. The ADA complained about the studies. By the late seventies early eighties there was certainly enough controversy that no self respecting dentist could consider amalgams safe. The ADA persisted. Dentists relied on the ADA.

In the face of study after study showing that the air inside a mouth with mercury fillings continually contains elemental mercury vapor the studies also showed that amalgams erode. Erosion contributes to toxic output. Having an amalgam means the recipient inhales mercury vapors 24 hours a day, 365 days a year.

I have three. I am more upset about the amalgams than I am about 13 or the colonic. I can hardly believe that no one said, "this is crazy". It is like the cigarette companies saying smoking does not cause cancer. This is worse though because this was Health Care Professionals not a corporation making harmful and false representations.

I trusted my dentist and now I have to have the mercury taken out of my mouth by none other than a dentist. My dentists have been nice people. I do not believe any dentist meant any harm to me except maybe the Air Force dentist when I was young. So we do what we do because people tell us that is what we should do. The dentists gave me amalgam fillings not because they were trying to hurt me. The dentists were trying to help me. The dentists were fixing my teeth. That is a helpful thing to do.

It would be hard to be a dentist. At least that is my impression. It takes a long time to be a dentist, i.e. four years of college, three years of dental school, some training thereafter and then work. All that education costs a lot of money. A dentist has devoted seven years of time in education and spent as much as several hundred thousand dollars to acquire the skills to become a dentist. I do not believe any person would expend resources to begin a practice with a goal of hurting people.

That may happen later when loans become due or problems at home develop, or years of patients saying, "I hate the dentist" reach the point that the Air Force dentist would tell my mother "Children do not feel pain when their cavities are filled." My mouth is little. When I was five I am sure it was much smaller. I have no idea how the dentist got his hand in my mouth to even drill. I remember his hands. His hands were hairy. I hope they were clean. I am not sure when dentists started wearing latex gloves but my Air Force dentist incident was years before the advent of latex gloves.

So we do what we are taught. Dentists were taught to fill teeth with amalgam fillings. Now I have mercury in my mouth and I need to get it out. But I am so caught up in the hairy handed Air Force dentist that I do not want to stress myself out by having the fillings removed and replaced. I will do it, just not now.

# 37

# MY LEFT BREAST

My left breast was never quite as big as my right breast. I am right handed and right side dominant so my left breast, like my left arm, is slightly smaller than their respective right side counter parts. But now my left breast is significantly smaller.

I have been afraid to look at my left breast. I looked at it a lot when it still had the nipple ring. I loved the nipple ring. The nipple ring was a circle of stainless steel with a small black onyx bead at the center. I thought it was cool. I never saw a tumor. I never felt a tumor. No one else felt a tumor.

I do not know how long the tumor had been in my left breast. Consequently I do not know how many people touched my left breast without feeling a tumor. I never felt it. I touched my left breast. I did exams. But I never felt a tumor. And I always admired the defiance of my left breast exemplified by the nipple ring.

It is a deadly combination to desperately care what other people think about me and at the same time be filled with defiance. I do care what people think about me. Most of my life I have cared more about what other people think about me than what I think about me.

My parents cared about what other people thought, about them, about all of us. My mother was the sixth of seven children. Her parents were Catholic. She was born in Alameda California, an island town adjacent to Oakland. In 1921, in Alameda when my mother was born there was no bridge connecting Alameda to the main land. I mention that only because when the Park Street Bridge, which still stands and is in use today, was opened, my mother carried the American flag leading her brownie troop across the bridge to commemorate the opening. I love that she did that. I love that because it is one of the few happy stories she tells of her childhood. So I tell and retell that story.

My mother's childhood was hard. She was born and raised in the depression years. Her father died when she was not quite a teenager. The family was poor after that. Her mother took a job as a seamstress at Magnin's department store in downtown Oakland. My mother ran the household. There was never enough money. There was hardly enough food. She attended Catholic schools because the nuns allowed it. They took pity on the poor Catholic family whose breadwinner met an untimely and tragic death from developing hiccups after an appendectomy. My grandfather started hiccupping shortly after surgery and would not or could not stop. The hiccupping tore the stitches, and led to internal bleeding and he died. My mother was in seventh grade when her father died and the nuns let her stay.

Every year at the beginning of the school year at my mother's Catholic school each student had to submit to a minor physical. The physicals were performed in the school auditorium. The physicals were routine enough. The nurse measured the student's weight and height, and took vital signs. The students wore uniforms. The girls including my mother wore white socks and saddle shoes. The physicals happened on the first or second day of school.

On the first day of school the year after my mother's father died my mother wore her uniform and clean white socks and shoes. She had two pairs of socks. One pair had a hole in the toes and the other pair did not. My mother worried which day the physicals would be done. She did not want to take her shoes off to be measured for height for the other people to see her wearing socks that had holes. She did not want others to see the holes in her socks because in her mind that would mean that they would all know how poor her family was.

The first day of school came and went without the physical being administered. My mother dressed for school on the second day and again put on the socks that were no longer clean but were without holes. Her mother intervened and made her take off the dirty socks and put on the clean socks with the hole. My mother hoped the physical would not be administered. She worried about the hole in the toe of her sock. All morning she worried. She hoped the physical would be done on day three when she would be wearing the holeless socks which would now be clean as her mother washed all the socks every night. My mother was not the only child in her family who had only two pair of socks. My grandmother washed socks every day. That is how my mother got caught by her mother. There were only six pairs to be washed and there were seven children.

My mother was too young to have thought of just giving the pair of socks that had the holes as her contribution to the daily seven pairs of socks-one pair from each child routine. That would have worked. My grandmother was not an expert on the condition of the socks just the number.

At noon on the second day the physical began. It was either a size order line or alphabetical order. Either way my mother was at the beginning of the line. Like me she is relatively small. My mother's last name, her maiden name is Carlson and like Canny, both begin with a C. Either way, like me, she was always near the front of the line.

She tried to be measured wearing her shoes. That made it worse and called more attention to her than had she just taken off her shoes. Now a nun commanded her to take off her shoes. My mother hesitated. The hesitancy was misinterpreted by the nun as defiance and the nun yelled at her bringing even more attention to her.

I imagine my mother's ears were red and her stomach knotted as each ensuing second brought on more shame. Shame that she had socks with holes, which actually sounds more plentiful than socks without holes, but she did not feel plentiful. The shame was so much more than the socks. She felt shame about being poor, about not having a father, about all that and then some.

She took her shoes off and stood on the scale. The school nurse saw her holes. So did the nun. I am not sure how many classmates saw the holes but in my mother's head everyone did and everyone knew that she was poor and could not afford to get another pair of socks without holes. She hated that experience. I hate that my mother had to have that experience. I wish that I could fill my mother's life with joyful experiences, and that she would never have to feel any pain. I am sure that she feels the same as for me.

As time passed for my mother, as she grew up, she became more and more able to protect herself from what other people thought-actually about what she thought other people thought. My mother was great looking. She became a flight attendant in the first International class for Trans World Airlines (TWA), the first year flight attendants were no longer required to be nurses. She traveled all over the world. One of my favorite pictures of my mother was taken in Egypt. My mother is sitting on a camel in front of a pyramid. She is about 23 years old. She was not thinking about holes in her socks when that picture was taken.

I believe my mother never wanted me to experience her hole in the socks feelings. I never had socks with holes in them. The irony is that the experience was never about socks. The story is about self acceptance and misplaced concern about what other people think. It is a lot easier to say I don't care what other people think sitting on a camel in front of a pyramid five thousand miles from home than it is to be 12 years old with holes in one's socks in front of the entire class. The person on the camel still did care what others think but since she felt good she believed anyone seeing her would be amazed at how far she had come and be impressed. Because my mother believed they would be impressed she did not care. But she did and so do I.

My mother did her best to have me escape a hole in the sock experience. I learned how to do pretty much everything before most of my peers. My mother always dressed me in clean clothes and fashionable clothes. I always looked like I fit in. My mother saw to that.

When I was 15 just after my freshman year in high school I told my mother that I thought there was something wrong with me. I could not describe much more than that. I had a difficult time at high school, Georgetown Visitation College Prep School for Young Ladies. I felt like I did not fit in. I could not figure out why I felt so out of place.

I did not tell anyone that is how I felt. All I could say is there is something wrong with me. My mother took me to the hospital at Fort Meyer for an examination. The doctor examined me. By all accounts he said I was exceptionally healthy. I was swimming competitively which meant swimming just about every day. I played other sports as well. I had just started drinking and smoking and denied both. The doctor could find nothing wrong with me.

The doctor asked me again, "What do you think is wrong with you?"

He had just examined me and could find nothing wrong so I believe he purposefully did not ask "What is wrong with you?" He already knew there was nothing wrong with me.

I told him that there is something wrong with the way I talk. I complained that my voice was too nasally. He seemed pleased and relieved that I could provide an identifiable pathology. He sent me to a speech pathologist. The appointment was arranged for a week or so off.

I felt relieved that there was someone who could help me. At this point I had become convinced that my speaking voice was the reason why I did not feel like I fit in. Again I never said to anyone that I felt as if did not fit in only that there was something wrong with me.

On appointment day my mother and I drove to Fort Meyer to pick up my medical records to take to the speech pathologist. The speech pathologist's office was at a different army hospital, Walker Reed. We did not look at my medical records. Although they were mine, about me, they somehow felt confidential, like they were none of my business.

I met with the speech pathologist. He was very nice. He listened to me speak. He asked what I thought was wrong with the way I spoke. I told him my voice was too nasally. I told him that my accent was weird. He told me, "Your accent is not weird. It is your accent."

As to the 'nasally' complaint he suggested I keep my voice lower and the nasalness would be gone. We practiced and in a few minutes it was gone. I asked if I needed more appointments. "No" he told me, "There is nothing wrong with your speech or your voice."

Instead of being happy I was distressed. I thought my voice was what was wrong with me. I had just learned it was not that and now I had no other idea what was wrong with me. The speech pathologist saw the distress on my face. The speech pathologist told me to look at my medical records.

He gave me the records. My mother and I got in the car. I opened the records. At about page seven or eight I saw an entry from Ryslip Air Force Base made when I was about five or six years old, sometime in 1960.

The doctor's notes recorded a routine physical examination and concluded I was in good health. There was an addendum. My mother had commented to the doctor that I liked to wear pants, cowboy boots and a pair of six shooters when not in my school uniform. That was all that was ascribed to my mother in the record. The doctor then noted in the record that he explained that such likes on my part were "phenomena of possible homosexual tendencies."

I read the few lines to my mother. I started screaming at her, "How could you?" I was not sure what a homosexual was or what homosexual tendencies are I just knew they were really bad. My mother yelled at the "fucking doctor" for misconstruing her observation of me, as it was true at the age of five, while in England I only liked to wear pants, cowboy boots and six shooters when not in my school uniform. Such choices could have easily been interpreted as American jingoism living in a foreign land, efforts to retain my American heritage as opposed to homosexual tendencies. My mother was as angry as I was. She was yelling as she drove. I was yelling as she drove though Walter Reed.

We drove by a trash can. She stopped the car. No one wore seat belts in those days including us. She stopped the car so hard we both bounced. My mother said, "Rip the page out of the records, tear it up and throw it in that garbage can."

There was no one around. I did what she said. I worried how many people had already read that. I worried that we would get caught for destroying a record. I worried more that if I did not throw it out all the rest of my life anyone who looked at the records might see that my mother's observations led to conclusions of homosexual tendencies by someone so important as a doctor.

That was my first true lesson in not understanding that I am terribly invested in what other people think of me and that the best option in controlling what other people think is to control what information is disclosed. In retrospect I feel worse for my mother about the experience because I think she worried that I was gay long before I read the hospital record.

I think my mother always worried about me. I think she never wanted me to experience the feelings that she felt when she took the physical with the holes in her socks. Ripping the page out of the medical records was my mother's version of giving me a new pair of socks. I am sure she meant to protect me.

The problem is that I turned out to be a homosexual. The doctor was right and my mother's confession to him of her observations made it appear that was her opinion. Even if it was her opinion, which it never was, she would never have said so; because it turns out I think it was her biggest fear. My biggest fear was not being accepted. So on that day that I tore the page out of my Air Force medical records my mother and I came to an understanding.

I was 15 years old and really had no idea what having homosexual tendencies meant, nor did I know what a homosexual was. I vaguely knew it was bad and terrible, so terrible I yelled at my mother for complaining about me, for giving information that led to conclusions about me that clearly was just as shocking to her as it was to me.

My mother said, "The doctor is an ass." She yelled it actually. We yelled a lot of things when she slammed on the brakes and ordered me to tear the entire page out of the records.

Once the page was torn up and in the trash can the whole issue disappeared. We never spoke of the page again. My mother says she does not remember. I do. She could have said, "There's nothing wrong with being gay." She could have said, "You're perfect however you are." She could have said, "This will be interesting. It is for you to know who you are. Be true to yourself."

None of that was said. None of it has ever really been said. I know my mother loves me. I know that my mother would do anything for me. I know that my mother has always done the very best she could for me. I know my mother sacrificed for me, and my brother, so that we would have an education and the best opportunities possible. But I also knew that my being a lesbian has stressed her out not because she does not love me, she does, but because she is worried about what other people think, maybe not just about me, but about us both.

It has taken years for me to be semi at peace with the notion that I am precisely who and how God intended me to be. My mother tried so hard for me to be normal. There was nothing my mother could do. Being a lesbian is normal for me.

But I digress from the real reason I am here in this discussion, and that is my left breast. The nipple ring is gone. I took it out shortly after the cancerous tumor was found. I do like that the mammogram photos show my left breast with the nipple ring, an x-ray of my left breast with a ring.

The x-ray photos remind me of my deceased dog Kailas' x-ray when she swallowed a fish hook. One afternoon Kailas and the puppies and Elly and I went walking on the beach and Kailas saw a fish and ate it. The fish was on a hook and had been bait that had been discarded by a fisherman. Kailas swallowed the fish and then realized it was a hook and tried to pull it out by pulling on the line with her paw. The hook got caught in her esophagus. We took her to the Emergency Pet Hospital and they x-rayed her. There in the middle of this massive mastiff dog's head and neck x-ray was a fish hook. The Vet did an endoscope and got it out. But it was terrible. My nipple ring and Kailas' fish hook are the best things I've ever seen on x-rays.

After I took my nipple ring out my left breast just looked like a left breast, or maybe just a breast. I am not sure you can tell a left breast from a right breast per se. For four months my left breast looked like a left breast. By looking at it no one could tell of the war that was raging inside it with chemo drugs attacking cancer cells. It just looked like a left breast. The rest of me looked bad. The bald head, pale, gray skin made it apparent that I was getting chemotherapy but my breast by itself looked just like a breast.

Then came surgery. The chemo had killed the cancer and Lora did a great job taking it out of my left breast. After surgery someone somehow got my breast in a bra that Velcroed shut. The Velcro bra went over the bandages which were over the incision. There was a bandage over the incision under my arm, in my left arm pit where the two lymph nodes had been taken.

I did not look at the bandages or the Velcro bra. I kept myself covered. After two days I took the Velcro bra off and showered. I did not look at my left breast or my arm pit. A few days later I went to Lora's for a post operation examination. Lora seemed pleased. I made a passing glance at my breast and saw some bruising and decided not to look further.

A few days later I had an appointment with Dr. Ekstrand and he looked at my breast. Dr. Ekstrand seemed impressed by Lora's work. I showed my left breast to anyone at the Cancer Center who cared to look. All viewers expressed admiration for Lora's work. I still did not look. I had worried about radiation. I think Brad worried that I would not do radiation and what it would do to my left breast that I was now afraid to look at.

I went to Seton Medical Center for my radiation therapy interview and examination. I talked to Dr. Barry Chaucer and he talked to me. Dr Chaucer seemed confident and competent. He examined me. Dr. Chaucer looked at my left breast. Like all the others he commented on the quality of Lora's work. I still did not look at my breast. I wanted to but was afraid to. Lora's good work meant part of me was missing. I was afraid to look to see just how much of me and my left breast was gone. In my head it was as if not looking meant the gone part, was still there.

I cannot see the missing part when I look down. The missing part is or was the underneath part of the breast. I did not look at my breast until Sanoviv. I have looked and looked at her over the past few days. In clothes no one can tell I had part of my left breast cut out. Naked there is a scar about two inches long. The scar runs laterally. One time when I saw Lora after the surgery she probed at the scabbing on the scar. There is no more scabbing. There is no more bruising. There is just a scar. A lot of the underneath part of my left breast is missing. Naked it is apparent part of my left breast was removed. I have stood in the mirror and looked at my left breast and my right breast. I have flexed and relaxed and I am now comfortable with my less than before scarred left breast.

The scar is better than the nipple ring. The scar is me. The left breast is me. When I was readied for radiation the technologist drew on me with a red magic marker (Sharpie). I joked that I am sure that the red Sharpie is organic and contains no carcinogens. She did not laugh. The irony of writing on myself with chemicals that contribute to cancer in order to cure cancer was not lost on me. I do not know how it is for them except they make the markings each and everyday and Sharpies were best for them which in turn means I will get the x-rays in the right places.

After I got marked up with the red Sharpie the technologist tattooed the areas of my left breast in four places. The tattoos are tiny, but nevertheless they are tattoos, and they surround my surgically diminished, cancer free left breast. The tattoos are tiny little lines. One tattoo is at the bottom of my pectoral muscle. Another tattoo is on my left side, parallel to my nipple. The third tattoo is on a stomach muscle just beneath my left breast and seems to be made randomly. That observation says more about my ignorance. The final and fourth mini tattoo is one inch above my sternum on the skin on the bone. My left breast is framed now by four tiny tattoos.

I may have lost a nipple ring but I gained four mini tattoos.

# 38

# RANDOM RANTINGS
# AND A FEW TIPS

The nipple ring was an act of defiance on the one hand and on the other it was an act of making art. Perhaps art is a form of defiance. But it was my art and my nipple ring and I love that I had a nipple ring. I had never really thought I would be brave enough to get a nipple ring and yet I did do it. I had thought though that it was possible that I would get cancer. Somehow I knew that I would have this experience. I never wanted the experience but on some weird level deep in my brain I knew that I would have this experience. It was not so much that I discovered or learned that I had cancer. I did not think that when my left nipple hurt where the ring was. I did not think that when I felt the lump in my right breast. It was sometime after that I realized that the cancer diagnosis was really more about remembering that I would have this experience. My body knew before my mind and my being knew. It is hard to explain. It feels like much of my life is not so much about discovering as it is remembering.

The philosophy of Aristotle comes to mind. I believe he taught that we do not learn but that we remember or something like that. Which leads me to believe then that anything is possible and that virtually anything I think is possible is possible as it relates to me. If I think I can get cancer, I could get cancer. If I think I could write a book, I could write a book. There are limits in that I can think I could run a marathon in under three hours but to make that happen would take far more work than I am willing to devote. But on a level of success and accomplishment my thoughts do control what I do and how I do it. So I will think that it is possible that I will not ever again have cancer. That is what I think. I will not have cancer again. I think I will eat right and sleep more and stress less and then I think it is possible that I will not get cancer again. Anything is possible and just as I thought on some deep level that I would have this experience. I also believe that I will not have this experience again. I have learned from this experience and I am finished with this lesson. That is what I think is possible.

When I was thinking about what is possible and what is not and all that, I started thinking about corporations. I do not know why. I just did. I suppose because someone thought such an entity was possible and now look at us some 100 years later. There are so many corporations. I remember being in law school and attending 'corporations' class. 'Corporations' was a required class. Family law was not. Now what does that say? The first thing out of the professor's mouth extolling the virtues of corporations was that the shareholders have no personal liability. That fact was the great part about corporations and why the corporation was therefore the preferred form of business organization.

I did not say anything. I just wrote that statement in my notebook and for years whenever I heard anything about a corporation I would think to myself how great the greatness of a corporation is in that the shareholders have no personal liability. It took getting cancer to appreciate how absolutely sociopathic the concept is. How could anything that does not take responsibility be good?

When I ask how food can be produced that is poison and harmful as done by food corporations the answer is there is no personal accountability to the owners of the corporation. The sole function of the corporation is to make money. The other exacerbating fact of life in the United States is that the agency created to regulate the Food Industry does not regulate the industry. It protects the industry. The only entity entitled to bring a lawsuit against any food producer for mislabeling food or not identifying food as required by law is the United States Government. That is the law. A consumer has no such right. That is insane. We have a system in place where the corporation has no personal responsibility of its owners and a regulatory agency that is controlled by corporations. It is one of those things that if any of us rationally thought about what is occurring we would stop it, if we had the power.

As consumers we do have power. What we buy is a political statement. Where we buy is a political statement. The point is if I do not buy from any corporation then I doubt that I will ever eat anything bad again. How is that for simplicity. And then I wonder can I even survive without buying food from a corporation and how sad is that. How sad to realize that food production is essentially in the hands of persons who are not accountable for what they produce.

Food subsides complicate matters. Corn is grown because it is profitable to grow because it is subsidized. Since it is grown it is used. So salmon is fed corn, which makes farmed salmon gray in color. Consumers do not want to eat gray fish because everyone knows salmon is pink. Gray salmon is gray because it is sick because it has been fed corn which salmon were not meant to eat. Rather than feed salmon what salmon were meant to eat, corporate fisheries that raise salmon put chemicals in the corn to turn the fish pink so that the consumer will think that they are eating wild salmon and healthy salmon, neither of which is true.

The USDA does not do anything about that and so more and more of us are getting cancer because we are being poisoned by what we eat. What I think is possible is that corporations and the shareholders must be held accountable for what they do. That is possible.

The benefit of a corporation is no personal liability to the shareholders. That is insane. Corporations' very existence is premised on lack of accountability. Corporations receive better tax treatment than individuals, and are not accountable.

The one thing we all have in common is that we are consumers. Not one person in this country, in this world, is not a consumer. We may vary in what we consume and how much we consume, but we all consume.

We consume food and water to survive. What food we consume varies but in order to live some food is consumed. I do not know what I am eating anymore. When farmers grew food, people grew food. I trusted that the farmers would provide quality food for two reasons. One, people are basically good and take pride in what they are doing and want to do what they do well. And two the product must be of a quality to bring back repeat business. If they produce an inferior product or a harmful product they are personally accountable in that they will fail due to lack of customers.

When a corporation grows food the primary concern is profit as well as long-term growth without the burden of accountability. So long as the product, whatever it is contributes to short term profit which contributes to long term growth, methods that may well lead to long term harm are undertaken because there is no accountability for the shareholders in the form of personal responsibility.

Shareholders can bring suits but cannot be sued as shareholders unless the corporate veil can be pierced. Corporations are a kind of cancer. They certainly have led to a society that produces cancer causing agents. Prevention is different than correction, unless you are a corporate drug manufacturer. It is insane. Fish fed grain. Cows fed grain-e coli result of infection resulting from being fed contaminated grain. Insane, absolutely insane.

A diatribe on corporations is not much help to me or anyone with cancer. Practical suggestions may be of more help. The best suggestion that I have heard about avoiding a cancer reoccurrence relates to changing the way that I live. Of course I would like to revolutionize society, but in the short run I need to be healthy enough to help with the necessary change.

Cancer likes an acidic environment. Consequently I must do all the things that change my body's chemical environment from acidic to alkaline. The trick for that is to begin each day by drinking organic squeezed lemon in hot water. It turns the PH of my body into alkaline. Adding cayenne pepper to the drink opens the capillaries and improves circulation. So instead of strong coffee I start my day with strong hot lemon.

During the day I no longer eat sugar. I have sworn off all of the candy bars, not because they are made by corporations, but because what they are made of. Corn Syrup, which is mass-produced, and now a part of most processed foods is bad for people. Corn syrup is just processed sugar and that is bad for people, which also means that cancer likes corn syrup because cancer thrives on sugar. Cancer is a cell mutation. Cancer likes other cell mutations. Processed foods are cell mutations. So I now try not to eat things that cancer likes. I do not want to give myself anything that cancer would enjoy, or that could give energy to cancer.

I try to eat whole foods that are organically grown as cancer does not like such good cells. Cancer seems to like genetic alterations so I also try to not eat anything that has been genetically altered. But that can be tricky as food labeling laws do not really require the corporation to tell us what it is they have done to the food. Take for example salmon as was discussed above. Domestically grown salmon are gray. The fish are gray because they are sick. They are sick because they are fed corn. The fish have been fed corn because corn is abundantly grown because of farm subsidy payments to corporations and the corporations need to sell it somewhere so the imprisoned fish on the corporate fish farm are fed corn. Now what fish actually eats corn? Imprisoned farm fed salmon are what eat corn. Really that is unbelievable. So the fish grow until they are harvested for distribution to the supermarkets. But they are gray salmon. Well actually they would have been gray salmon but the super market chains had already realized as had the salmon farmers that consumers do not want to buy gray salmon, as everyone knows that salmon is pink. So the solution for the growers of the corn fed salmon is to give the salmon chemicals that cause the salmon meat to turn from gray to pink. The chemicals are known carcinogens. The salmon looks like wild salmon in that it is pink. The supermarket under federal law is not required to identify the product as corn fed, farm raised, and chemically ingested dyed fish. The point is eating can be problematic. But I try very hard to eat food that is God's food and not corporate product.

The other tricks to avoid cancer are to get plenty of rest and sleep. That is a hard task for me. That task includes sleeping in a dark room. That has been hard for me because I have always been a little afraid to go to sleep. I still do not know what that is about but for years I have slept with a television on. I have since learned that is bad so I have stopped, except when I have not.

I also think that what any of us does has to be what we think is best for us. The problem is that so much of what I had thought was good for me is actually not. So I have really had to undergo a thorough examination of what I thought was correct and then critically examine what I thought. Believe me that takes up a lot of time. Luckily I have the time.

# 39

# JUST WHEN I THOUGHT EVERYTHING WAS GETTING BETTER

November 6, 2007

Just when I thought everything was getting better and everything was getting better I had to reevaluate. When I got home from Sanoviv I began radiation. That has been hard. Even with the four mini tattoos the radiation technicians drew other lines on my left breast with a magic marker. These are big lines and big dots. I asked them again if the magic marker contained cancer-causing materials. The techs said no one had ever asked that before. I can hardly believe that. But they said the magic- marker, that they call a sharpie, says on the side that it is Nontoxic. I do not know what nontoxic means. I doubt that the person who wrote it knows what it means either. I suppose I feel better about that than reading that it is toxic. But I am still not sure I know what nontoxic means.

I hardly know what anything means as language has become so distorted. I just learned that "cage free chickens" does not mean that the chickens are not in a cage. It means they are in a cage that is big enough so that they can walk, however slightly, in the cage. So I do not know what nontoxic means, nor do I know what it was intended to mean. I only know there are little magic marker Xs and lines all over portions of my left breast and the Xs help the techs line up where they are going to have the machine shoot radiation through my left breast.

Radiation makes me tired. I did not write at all after the first week because I was too tired. I am surprised that it made me tired. The second week does not seem so bad. Each day I get a little more hair and can almost pass as someone who was not treated for cancer. A woman's bald head is a definite indicator of chemotherapy. I have a GI Jane look going. I like it. I am back to work on a limited basis. I yell a lot at work so I am mildly disappointed that I have not changed very much. I am sure the people at my office are far more disappointed.

Woody and I went sailing on Saturday with Lora and Dan. We had a perfect day. Woody is a great sailor. I called her my sailor girl all day and we laughed. I felt like everything was turning around. The day was sunny and hot for a November day in the bay. I felt great in spite of a headache. I felt hope. We sailed under the Bay Bridge and somehow it did not look so scary. Woody had a good time. We all did.

I had a slight case of the Monday Morning Working Girl Blues on Monday. I was nice but had a bit of self- pity. Woody had an ultrasound scheduled as she has had some abdominal pain. The week before Woody had successfully passed her ob/gyn exam. I had not told her in any great detail about my failed pelvic exam. She did not fail. She passed. But Woody still had abdominal pain since the day of my surgery. Woody had been experiencing pains in her abdomen for some two months. At the time I did not think of her pains as two months of abdominal pains. I have sort of lost track of what two months means. Since her pelvic exam was perfect the doctor ordered an ultrasound. The ultrasound would answer the question as to why Woody had been in pain for over two months.

On the day of the ultrasound I went to court and the Department of Motor Vehicles. That is a whole other place and story. I did not miss going there when I was sick. I came home to see Woody after her ultrasound and also get some food. Woody was not home. I forgot to eat. I forgot to take my vitamins. I wondered where Woody was. I waited and I worked. I went to radiation. Once I got to the hospital I realized that I had not eaten and that I had not heard from Woody. I decided to eat a salad at the hospital cafeteria. The cafeteria was bordering on filthy and there were mostly unhealthy foods for sale. The irony was not lost on me- that the hospital serves food in a way that could make one sick. I decided never to eat at the cafeteria again and to just not think about what I had eaten. I wondered about Woody, really I worried.

After radiation I saw Victor Conte and we discussed Balco matters. I returned to the office to yell at people and review a medical malpractice complaint that I want to file. I took a call from a client in China. I yelled at my brother who now works for me as he awaits his bar results. I wondered about Woody, really I worried. Now that was a miserable time.

When I got home Woody had made dinner for us. Monday night football was on. The Steelers were up 35 to 0 before the first half. That was shocking. We had dinner and watched the game. Everything seemed so much in order and okay that I assumed everything was good with Woody and there was no problem with the ultrasound.

Sometime after dinner, in a very nonchalant way, Woody told me that her ultrasound had revealed a 9 centimeter (4 inch) tumor on her left ovary. She told me that the hospital had called her back to give blood for a blood test to see if the tumor is cancerous. Woody said that she returned to the hospital and gave blood. Woody told me that she had called Lora. Woody said that Lora had called Michelle and that Michelle my gynecologist had called Woody as well. All of the doctors concluded that the tumor might be cancerous and it might not be. We just will not know for a few days.

When Woody finished giving me the forgoing information we both laughed. We are both incredulous. It is not funny. But the last six months have been terrible and I do not want Woody to have to go through what I just went through. I do not want to go through what Woody had just gone through watching me go through what I had just gone through. I told Woody that is what happens when our combined ages are over 100. We laughed some more. Then I held Woody and we hugged. For a long time we hugged and did nothing more. We did not say a lot. This is just unbelievable.

Whatever is in Woody's guts on her left ovary is what it is. It is just waiting for us to find out what it is. It knows. We don't. It will take a few days. Woody has a CAT scan tomorrow. I am supposed to have the tooth fixed that I broke in Sanoviv. And I wonder how weirder any of this can get.

# 40

## WOODY'S CAT SCAN

I still cannot believe that Woody has to have a CAT scan. Woody has Kaiser Health Insurance. We had talked about her switching to my Blue Cross. But we had procrastinated. Woody will have to deal with this with Kaiser. She does not really have a choice at this point. Woody did have a choice as to the flavor of the barium to drink in preparation of the CAT scan. I think Woody picked the unflavored barium because she remembered how much I had complained about the banana flavored barium Woody picked the unflavored barium. Joan took Woody to the CAT scan because I had a dentist appointment to fix my broken tooth.

While Woody was getting her CAT scan, I was getting laughing gas while Jennifer my dentist fixed my broken tooth. I got laughing gas for two hours, which is way too long to just get up and leave. But I did just get up and leave. I was worried about Woody. I wanted to know what the CAT scan revealed. I tried to walk around the block and got lost. I was still so high. I went to Lisa's office and we called her partner, Michelle the gynecologist and arranged for Woody to see Michelle to show her the films from the CAT scan and the ultra sound.

I drove over to St. Luke's Hospital to meet Michelle and Woody. I was still high. We looked at the images. I had learned a lot from studying the breast images of my left breast. When looking I learned to focus on the tumor. Looking at Woody's films I saw that the tumor is large, even on the screen the tumor looks large. Woody's ovarian tumor is bigger than my cancerous breast tumor. It is big enough that based on its size alone Michelle confided to me "it is worrisome". I thought anything that big has got to be worrisome. Anything growing in my girlfriend's uterus is worrisome. Its very presence is worrisome. What I really wanted to know is whether or not it is a cancerous tumor.

Apparently we will find out whether or not the tumor is cancerous when Woody is operated on. It could be benign. It could be cancerous. There is a blood test for ovarian cancer. It is called a CA 125 test. I have no idea what CA 125 means. I just know that if the number is high that is a strong indication that the tumor is cancerous. The tumor itself is defined, or at least appears so from the ultrasound. 'Defined' means that it has a definite shape. There does not seem to be a lot of blood flow into the tumor. Those two things are good, leading to an inference that the tumor is more likely benign. But the tumor could also still be cancerous. The CAT scan showed nothing remarkable. That too is good, meaning the only thing growing in Woody's guts is the 9 centimeter tumor.

I am getting radiation everyday at 2:30 p.m. at Seton medical Center. Any radiation patient, including me, gets to park in doctors' parking lot. All of the radiation people are great. Everyone smiles and is professional and very low key. I do not mind going. Maybe I should mind. Maybe I am not smart enough to know that radiation is difficult. The Xs they put on my breast with a magic marker are still there, along with the lines. They do not seem to wash off.

Every day I park in the physician's parking lot. I go into the lobby and say hello to Lois. Lois makes a notation in the computer that I have arrived. I go back to the waiting room area. I get a clean gown and take off my clothes from the waist up. I put on the hospital gown opening in the back. I never wait more that a few minutes before I am called into the room where I get zapped.

In the zapping room there is a giant machine that shoots radiation. There is a narrow table that I lay down on. They put a pillow under my legs. On the table are clean white sheets. After I lay on the table I open the gown removing my left arm from the gown so that my left breast is exposed. My left breast has the four small tattoos around it and several magic marker Xs, two of which are big. My breast has scars from the surgery and Xs on the left and right side from the nipple. My poor left breast has been through so much.

Woody has gone through so much and now she has to go through the surgery of removing the unknown tumor from her ovary and then maybe have her ovary and her other ovary removed and perhaps suffer a complete hysterectomy. The tumor is so big and unknown that we doubt that they can remove it laporoscopically. A laporoscope is a device that is inserted into the guts and basically cuts the item to be removed out and does not require a large incision in the guts. The laporoscope in Woody's case would be inserted into her belly button and the surgeon would work through there. Because no one knows what the tumor is, it is deemed not safe to attempt to remove it laporoscopically. That means Woody has to get cut open, much like having a cesarean section.

I never saw this coming. Neither did Woody. And now here we are. Woody's scar is going to be much bigger than mine if they have to cut her open. The recovery time for the proposed surgery is 6 to 8 weeks, sometimes longer. The proposed surgery date is the day before Thanksgiving, which means that we won't be going to Houston for Thanksgiving. Woody will be in the hospital and so will I. The protocol for a cancerous ovarian tumor is removal and not necessarily chemotherapy. I don't want Woody to have cancer. I don't want Woody to have to undergo chemotherapy, for her sake and for mine. For both of our sakes I do not want Woody to have cancer.

Woody's CA 125 test came back and the result was 64. That is slightly elevated but not elevated enough to conclude that the tumor is cancerous and not low enough to conclude that it is not. So we wait.

# 41

## HOW COULD I BE SO WRONG ABOUT SO MANY THINGS

How did I ever believe that food in a box is okay? We eat poison. In the name of money, which no one really owns, we are told to eat food that is really poison. Food in a box and processed food cannot be good for us. The processing robs the food of its nutritional value. Then for flavor and to preserve the processed food, chemicals are added to the processed food. Adios to the nutritional value and hello to the harmful active ingredients, all in a box. I hate going into super-huge supermarkets because they are filled with super poisons called processed foods.

The funny part is that neither Woody nor I ate all that many processed foods. I ate more than Woody. I drank far more than Woody, far more than most people drink in their lifetime. I ate McDonald's. I ate Big Macs, quarter pounders with cheese, french fries, and fake milkshakes throughout my teens and twenties. We had meat every night for dinner when I was growing up. My mother thought she was giving us good nutrition. My mother made Kool Aid for us. We had Good Humor ice cream every day in the summer. But overall my mother fed us real food, not processed food. My mother watched her weight and watched our weight. We exercised a lot as children.

Woody had pretty much the same diet as I did when she was growing up. Our parents thought what they were feeding us what was good for us. They believed what they were told. Our parents bought food from the store and bought processed foods thinking that if it was sold that it had to be good for a person and that it certainly would not be bad for anyone as how would anyone sell something that would be bad. That was the late fifties and sixties. There just was not the variety and abundance of processed foods as there are now. Woody's mother served them meat, potatoes, salad, and various vegetables. That was then. Now the traditional American meal is not good for anyone. Not because the concept is wrong, but because the food that we buy at the store is poison.

Cows that are raised for beef are injected with steroids and growth hormones and are fed corn. They are slaughtered and served to us before they can develop cancer. The executed cows are sliced up and put in clean packages so we are led to believe that the meat is clean and pure, that it did not even really come from a living being. I love steak. But how can I eat steak when I know the steak is filled with poison. I cannot. I should have known better. We all should know better. It is so insane that none of us thinks about what we eat and where what we eat comes from.

I have decided as a general rule I will not eat food from a box. I will not eat McDonald's, Burger King, Taco Bell, Wendy's, Carl's Junior, Kentucky Fried Chicken, or Jack in the Box ever again. The funny part is I have an emotional attachment to each one of those fast food chains. I have fond memories of my first McDonald's hamburger. In some odd way I have found comfort in all of those chains. I went to McDonald's in London the day it opened in 1976. The marketing people clearly did a great job. I am an educated woman who just went through months of chemotherapy. I should know better. Nevertheless I am sad that I am giving up McDonald's. I should be angry that I ever got attached. I had not even realized that I was attached. I guess that is precisely what the marketing people had intended. How humbling it is to realize I am such a predictable consumer.

I have decided that I won't eat anything from any large chain store. The economies of scale of purchasing result in the purchase of bulk materials that for the most part are not organically grown. Mass produced produce has been sprayed and fertilized and harvested and sprayed and transported. Megastores sell a lot of produce obtained from industrial farms where production goals are geared more towards quantity not quality. Mass production is the goal. They grow a lot, in whatever way they can, to make a lot, a lot of what- a lot of money. From the producers' perspective more is better. It is better for them but not for me or for any consumer. I now know better. From now on, no more food from a box for Woody and me.

I would rather think about food than worry about Woody. But I am worried.

# 42

# MEETING WOODY'S SURGEON

Woody and I met her gynecological oncologist surgeon on Tuesday, November 13, 2007 at the downtown San Francisco Kaiser Hospital. We drove in Woody's new car. Woody drove and I gave directions. Neither of us did either thing particularly well. We were each preoccupied. I went to radiation early in the morning so that I could go with Woody to meet the surgeon. The radiation does not seem to do anything to me other than I have a terrible sore throat and am not getting better. I have been sick for a few days. I may just have the flu or I may be sick from radiation. The radiation doctors say that I have the flu. There are no burns on my skin. But something is wrong with me as I have a fever of 102 or 103. I am sick. I told them at radiation that I am sick. Although they were concerned that I am sick they are clearly more concerned that I complete my radiation protocol. I got more radiation. After radiation I came home and rested. I waited until the last possible minute to get dressed in court clothes to accompany Woody to the Kaiser in San Francisco to meet the gynecological oncological surgeon.

His name is Ramey Littell. I checked on him. He trained at Massachusetts General Hospital. By all accounts he is really good at what he does. He is well liked and well respected. We were nervous about meeting him. Woody and I bickered about parking and where the building was and where we were going. But it was really lame, nothing like the commotion I used to create. We eventually got to the right building and the right floor and waited. The nurse called us. We were escorted to a room where the nurse told Woody to undress. Woody balked but eventually relented. Then Woody lay on the table with the extendable stirrups, naked except for the paper gown open in the back. We waited and Woody got cold. I covered her in her jacket. I was glad that I had a heavy wool suit on as my fever was soaring. I was freezing while we were waiting.

We joked. We waited. No one ever told us that Dr. Littell was prompt. The funny part was that Woody had asked the nurse if we would have to wait. The nurse indignantly said, "no, of course not." We knew she was wrong. We had to wait.

Eventually there was a knock at the door. We each knew it was Dr. Littell. He announced himself and came into the room. He was very cute. Dr. Littell has a goatee, and short hair, brownish with a few specks of gray. He wore a lab coat over good wool pants and great shoes. I wore court clothes in an attempt to look powerful. Regardless of my intent I did look well dressed. The doctor noticed. He had no choice.

His way was welcoming. Woody's way was exactly the opposite. Dr. Littell said, " I see in your chart that you said you preferred a woman." We offered the explanation that we knew that the woman surgeon was on medical leave. I told him that we had learned that he is very skilled in laporoscopic surgery so perhaps it was better. Woody was the ice queen. Woody was scared. I was scared that we were going to freak out the doctor. Dr. Littell offered to Woody, "you can ask me anything you want." Woody immediately responded, "How old are you?" The question surprised him. The question surprised me. Woody's tone was not friendly, but it was not hostile either.

Dr. Littell answered, "That is rather a personal question." But before he could finish Woody had added "you want to stick your fingers inside me. I think I have the right to know how old you are." Woody had a point there. He knows how old Woody is. He does intend to put his fingers inside her vagina and up her rectum. That is pretty personal. But they were at an impasse.

I am not sure what I said except I started babbling about everyone should want young doctors and old lawyers and that I am a lawyer and I just had breast cancer that is why my hair is so short. My hair is so short not because I am butch and bold in my hair style but rather because my hair fell out because of chemo. I babbled that my oncologist was young and he told me how old he was and that young doctors are good, better than young lawyers. I also kept talking about my hair, that my hair is just starting to grow back.

I babbled that I just had surgery and the day that I had surgery Woody had terrible pains and I thought she was having stress pains, little did I realize that she was feeling pain from the cystic mass that had brought us to him. I told Dr. Littell that Woody had been so great with me when I went through the whole horrible miserable past six months. I talked until I ran out of breath. If I had not been sick I could have talked much more, but my flu probably worked to everyone's benefit because I can go on and on. Because I was sick that was all I could say.

Somewhere in all the babble Woody relaxed and Dr. Littell relaxed and we were all good to be together. Dr. Littell reviewed the ultrasound and the CAT scan with us. He showed us images and explained various theories. Dr. Littell ultimately concluded that he believed the growth was more likely than not, not cancer, and that he was hopeful he could remove the growth laporoscopically. He ordered a colonoscopy and a MRI. We discussed options for well over an hour and a half. By the end of the meeting I think we all felt really good about one another.

As soon as we left the hospital my fever skyrocketed. Woody was pleased so I was pleased. I did not care about my now higher fever. We drove home in Woody's new car. We fed the dogs when we got home and decided a celebration was in order. We drove south on Highway 1 for Indian Food in Miramar. Indian food sounded good to me. Something hot and spicy, like Indian food, as if somehow the heat of the food would reverse my increasing fever sounded great to me. The restaurant was closed. We kept up our good cheer.

We drove to Bernal Heights and went to the Nepalese restaurant called Little Nepal. We called our friends Anna and Carla to join us. Carla was working on a paper for school but Anna came over. Carla had been Chief Inspector in the San Francisco Building Department until the politics became too much. She took a leave of absence to return to UC Berkeley to finish her degree. She has one year to go from the three she had spent at Cal almost twenty years ago. Carla is my very favorite coed. Anna is a wedding photographer and just did a photo shoot with Woody. Anna brought her computer. She showed us her photos of Woody. They are amazing. Woody looks like Woody. Woody looks great. The photos are amazing, so our dinner was so fun. My fever was hotter than the food.

I still had no idea how sick I was. My fever was back up over 103. My throat was sore. But I was so relieved that Dr. Littell was great and optimistic and that Woody was pleased with him, I forgot about how sick I am.

# 43

# EVERYTHING HAPPENS IN GOD'S TIME

On Wednesday I did radiation again. I did not work. I told my staff what to do. I did not return phone calls. I ached and slept and I coughed and coughed and coughed. I wondered if I should see a doctor. I saw a doctor, several doctors, at radiation but no one seemed that concerned about my coughing. They were more concerned about eradiating any trace of cancer that may be left on my left breast.

On Thursday November 15, 2007, I was sicker. I slept and watched Matlock and went to radiation. I did not work. I did not return phone calls. I coughed and coughed and coughed. My fever fluctuated between 101 and 103 plus.

It was on that day Thursday, November 15, 2007, that I remembered yet again what I should never ever forget- that everything happens in

God's time. I went into radiation without my telephone. There were just a few messages on my voicemail when I went in to radiation. These were the same few messages that I had been too sick and too weak to listen to. It was not so much that I did not have the ability to listen as much as the fact that even after listening I really did not have the ability to do anything about that which I had just heard.

Radiation takes only about twenty minutes. I went in about 2:30 pm. I got radiated. Dr. Chaucer examined me and expressed concern about my flu and my fever. Rather than stay and discuss my health care options with Dr. Chaucer, who was attempting to do just that, I felt a very strange compulsion to leave, that I was missing something. So I did. I just left.

I returned to my Cadillac Escalade. I love that car. I always wanted a Cadillac. I was too shy at first to get a Cadillac so I got a Chevy Tahoe, actually two of them, not at the same time, but one after another, until some four years ago when with the support of Woody I got what I wanted and got a Cadillac Escalade. My Cadillac Escalade is gold with a tan leather interior with wood trim and a Bulgari clock. I love that I drive a car that has a Bulgari clock. The Escalade is great to drive, very luxurious, and very big. It does not get the greatest gas mileage but it is great in the snow and has always been great for carrying the mastiffs. It can go anywhere and be perfect. A Cadillac is always perfect.

When I got back to the Escalade I checked my phone just like I always do. The voicemail said my phone's voicemail was full. That was odd. In one half hour I had received more then 30 voicemails. Either something had happened or someone who works with me has gotten obsessive. I started the car and started listening to my voicemail. I turned on the radio. The radio gave me the information that I needed to understand why I had received all of the phone calls.

Barry Bonds had been indicted for several counts of perjury and one count of obstruction of justice.

I drove home trying to reach Mark Geragos. Mark Geragos was Greg Anderson's attorney of record. I wanted to speak with Mark to make sure that Mark had arranged for Greg's release. Truly no arrangements should need to be made. Greg should be ordered released automatically as the indictment concludes the power of the subpoena that formed the basis of the contempt proceedings authorizing Greg's imprisonment. In other words I believed indicting Barry Bonds meant that Greg Anderson had to be released. The Government could either release Greg or we would have to prepare a motion asking the Court to release Greg. Such a motion had been prepared months ago and all had simply been waiting for the right time to file such a motion. The motion was done before I knew that I had cancer.

I never saw Barry's indictment coming at this time. I had speculated that Barry would get indicted. I just did not think it would be now. The United States Senate had just the day before confirmed Michael Mukaskey as the new Attorney General. Joseph Rusinello had just been nominated to become the U.S. Attorney for the Northern District of California. I thought that all of the newly appointed or soon to be appointed lawyers would have to ruminate more about what to do. Instead, out of the blue, the indictment was announced. I am trying to get Mark to have him call and verify that Greg would be released. I was sure that Mark's phone had to be ringing off the hook with every major media outlet seeking his sound bite. I was getting my share of calls as well, enough to fill my voice mail.

Eventually Mark and I reached each other. We talked and he agreed to call the Assistant U.S. Attorneys who in turn agreed to prepare a release order for Greg. With that I was off to Dublin Federal Prison to get Greg. I called the Prison and told them that I was on my way to pick up Greg. The operator sounded a bit confused. I know I sounded hoarse and coughed a lot. I had a fever and was sick. But there was no way that I was going to do anything other than get Greg. I had originally planned for us to wear Cancer Sucks t-shirts but I had not had them made, as I did not think that I would need them until January 2008.

Clearly I was wrong. I had thought the Government would wait to indict Barry until the very end of the grand jury's term as well as closer to the eighteen month maximum term of confinement for Greg. I was glad I was wrong. I did not have time to get the t-shirts. I wanted to get over the Bay Bridge before traffic became unbearable. I thought about changing into a suit and then changed my mind. There was no one for me to impress anyway. I have had my picture taken lots of times in a suit. I have been on television lots of times in a suit. I still did not have very much hair. Even in a suit I still look like someone who has undergone breast cancer treatment. Not even a suit can take that look away. So instead I decided to accentuate the obvious and simply wear what I wore to radiation.

I decided that what I was wearing was perfect. I was wearing very old blue jeans, soft and faded with purple Ugg boots and t-shirts covered with a green hooded sweatshirt with a giant V on the back and discreet writing on the left breast on its front saying "VISITATION". The sweatshirt was from my high school, Georgetown Visitation College Preparatory School for Young Ladies. I think they now say something more politically correct than young ladies, but that is what they said when I went there.

It seemed very funny to me that I would be photographed in a GVC sweatshirt. It is funny that me in a GVC sweatshirt would become the image that would appear in newspapers, and news clips, and the internet all over the country, even the world, for that one day. I could have picked anything to wear and I picked a GVC sweatshirt. Apparently I am still trying to impress the nuns.

I took calls on my cell phone and drove like a maniac. I used every short cut I knew to cut through the City and get on the Bay Bridge to get across the Bay. The drive was a blur, part from adrenalin and fever and part from distraction. I did several radio interviews as I drove. I talked to the prison a few more times. I made an agreement with the various television stations that I would stop on the way in and answer their questions, but on the way out Greg and I would not stop nor take any questions. I had no idea how sick I was.

Outside of the prison on the side of the road there was a mike stand set up with mikes from all of the various media outlets. There were lots of news trucks from all of the area television stations, as well as national cable stations. All the trucks had their antennas up. Flood lights were set up to illuminate the mike stand area. The reporters were dressed up and ready to go. Camera people milled about. They were waiting for me. Maybe not me in particular, but somebody to deliver some sound about the release of Greg Anderson. I could give them that. I drove up in my Escalade and parked.

Some of the reporters were surprised by my appearance, not the sweatshirt, but by my very short hair. People may hear that someone has undergone cancer treatment. I am sure that they had all heard I had undergone cancer treatment. But seeing the person is far more shocking than hearing about it. Seeing me is rather shocking. I looked like someone who had just done dose dense chemotherapy for four months, and who was undergoing radiation. In other words I looked like shit.

Then I started taking the reporters' questions. My voice was hoarse. I sounded resolute and impassioned but I still look like I had just undergone chemotherapy. I suppose that is my point. I have just finished chemotherapy and cancer sucks. But when all is said and done we all just do what we do. For me that meant driving out to prison to pick up Greg. I talked and talked and answered questions respectfully and candidly and when my voice would not allow another sound to be eked out I declared that the conference was over and went to the prison to get Greg.

I parked the car in the prison guards' lot because I did not have the energy to park and walk from the visitor's lot. I walked into the prison. I recognized all of the many people who I have been seeing and talking to over the past year and several months. Mr. Kubitz the Public Affairs Officer greeted me as did Greg's counselor and a few of the guards. I could see Greg. We were in adjacent fish bowls, separated by bullet-proof glass and a prison door. Greg had shaved but not had time for a haircut. I knew that because his face was clean-shaven and his hair was wild. We looked at each other. We were waiting for some other official in the process to conclude the release process so Greg could come into my fish tank and then leave.

The Prison Officials asked me if I brought clothes for Greg. I had not. I thought Greg still had the clothes he had worn when he turned himself into the prison on November 20, 2006 after the Ninth Circuit Court of Appeals had denied his appeal and ordered his return to prison. That was not a fun day. The Court of Appeals had issued its ruling. It was disappointing to say the least. Greg had been released some 47 days earlier on a rainy day by order of Judge Alsup at the behest of an earlier decision by the Court of Appeals. It was very dramatic. Mark Geragos and Justin Goodwin had left the federal Court House and walked in the pouring rain down to Market Street to buy Greg some sweats so that he could leave with us from the Court. The US Marshall's Service would not allow Greg to leave the building in his prisoner's garb. I waited in the holding cell visitor's room with Greg. The room makes me claustrophobic. I had cancer in my left breast then but I did not know it.

Mark and Justin came back with sweats. Greg was given the newly purchased sweats after the Marshals' inspected the clothes for weapons. Greg changed out of his prison uniform and into the newly purchased sweats. We all left together. There were lots of pictures taken of all of us. That was a fun day. Returning Greg to the prison was the opposite of the mania of that day. On November 20, 2006 Greg and I ate lunch together before his turn in time of 1 p.m. Greg had grilled chicken. He always has grilled chicken. We ate lunch. We tried to be cheerful. We failed. We were simply resigned. Greg wore casual clothes that day. Greg carried an orthopedic pillow and a doctor's prescription for the pillow when he walked into prison that day.

On the day Greg had to turn himself back into prison we drove into the prison in the Cadillac Escalade. I parked the car. One of the Prison Security Trucks driven by a prison guard drove up to us and asked what we were doing. I explained that Greg was turning himself in, in accordance with the Court's Order. The prison guard got excited. He grabbed for his walkie-talkie. He told us not to move and that he needed to call for back up. In an excited voice he called for back up. I reminded him that we were there to turn Greg in and we were not trying to escape, that we had just driven there. He again told us not to move. We ignored him and walked into the prison. We had walked into the building at least five minutes before his back up arrived.

When Greg surrendered to the prison that day they took his clothes and gave him the same uniform that he was not allowed to leave the federal building wearing. The guard said they would keep his clothes. I said good. But now the clothes were gone. So Greg sat in the very same fishbowl vestibule wearing prison clothes while I was waiting for Greg in the very same room that the guard said they would keep Greg's clothes and in the same room that they were now asking me whether or not I had brought clothes for Greg.

I explained to the prison officials that I thought Greg would be dressed in what he had arrived in on November 20, 2007 to leave. The prison staff could not find those clothes so they gave Greg other clothes. I thought Greg looked good. In some ways he looked better than I did. Greg certainly had more hair.

Greg and I were separated by the triple thick plate glass that had separated us for the past year. Greg was pacing and chatting. I was pacing and chatting. We each spoke with various prison officials. I worried about Greg, about what would come after this. For one year, Greg had been locked up at Dublin. Greg had missed Thanksgiving and Christmas, his birthday, his son Cole's birthday, the birthdays of all his loved ones, all of Cole's basketball, soccer, and baseball games. Greg has not been to the gym for some 52 weeks, locked in that shithole prison. I get confused as to why, but never as to how long.

Finally the processing was complete. The watch commander explained to me that they did not have to release Greg as the Order just said that Greg is "ordered released." He had tried that reasoning on me when I had called initially explaining that since the Order did not specify a date he took that to mean that they could wait until tomorrow to release Greg. I explained why I thought his interpretation was flawed. I think he wanted me to thank him for releasing Greg in the evening instead of the morning. I did thank him. I was polite. I also had decided that for whatever reason if they refused to release Greg that I would go out and give another press conference explaining that they would not release Greg until tomorrow because they are mean and oppressive and over bearing and that this is how our Government operates sometimes. The description sounded suspiciously like cancer to me. I would have welcomed the opportunity to rage at anything.

Greg and I did not walk out together as I had fantasized over the many months that I had anticipated this day. I first started to dream

of Greg's release on the day I brought Greg back. At that time I never thought that I would have cancer. I never thought that I would go through chemotherapy. I never dreamed that I would be bald. I forgot about all that as we left. When they let us leave we just walked out. Greg was carrying all of his belongings in a bag. Greg's face was hair free. His dreadlock Mohawk had grown out. Now Greg's hairdo looked similar to a mullet. We both laughed about that.

Just outside the prison under a streetlight were photographers. It was dark and the distance was several hundred yards. But the pictures taken of us ended up in the New York Times, New York Daily News, and every major newspaper in the United States. The San Francisco Chronicle had a photographer positioned at the gate and pictures were taken as we drove out. That was a much better picture. Many, many of my friends and acquaintances saw this photograph. Many called to tell me that they loved my short hair cut. I looked happy in that picture as I had a big smile on my face. I like that picture. I like that the picture is of me and Greg in my Cadillac Escalade. I am sure the Escalade likes it as well.

Pictures tell a thousand stories and then they don't. The picture did not tell that my fever was over 103. The picture did not tell that Greg was in shock. The picture did not tell that even as we were driving out of the Federal Prison the United States Attorney's Office had already started planning on how they would continue to pressure Greg. For that brief moment we were just happy. We ate at a Black Angus Restaurant. Greg ate with metal knifes and forks for the first time in 51 weeks, some 358 days. Greg ate what he wanted for the first time in some 1100 meals. He ate food that was not spoiled, that was cooked according his wishes. Food that is served in prisons is terrible. Often times it is purchased because expiration dates have passed and the food is thus very cheap. It is barely food. Greg worked in the kitchen so that he could get occasional decent food. We had a great time at dinner. Afterwards we were off to see his son Cole and Greg could go home to see his wife.

Cole was ecstatic and showed Greg every single new toy, bat, glove, shoe, anything and everything that he had gotten in the year Greg was imprisoned. It was fun. The hardest part about taking Greg home was avoiding the news trucks that were parked around Greg's apartment complex. By this time my fever was over 103. I had no business driving.

The craziness continued for days. It still continues. It will until it won't. I just kept getting sicker and sicker. I did an interview for the New York Daily News because my dear friend Rosemary Breslin had written for the Daily News years ago. Rosemary died a few years ago. I miss Rose so I agreed to do the interview in the hopes that the reporter knew Rosemary. I wanted to talk with Rosemary but obviously I could not so I thought speaking with someone who knew Rosemary would suffice. The reporter Christian Red did not know Rose, only of her, but that was good enough.

The interview was in the New York Daily News and a second story ran a few days later. I called it a living obituary not for any reason other than when the first story ran my fever had increased to 104. I had been given antibiotics that I was allergic to and was now vomiting every bit of bile and fluid left in me. I was dehydrated. I thought I was dying because I was dying. For the first time in the whole cancer chronicle I actually had the thought that I was dying, probably because for the first time in the process I was.

I hardly understood except that I understood that it was the small subtle things that slowly accumulated to the point that I was dying. I was still living, but the pendulum was swinging more towards the not keep living side than the getting better side. I was alone in my room in the middle of the night. Manaswar, my big mastiff dog, lay next to me on my bed. She watched me cough and wheeze. She looked worried. I felt worried. This was my Thanksgiving week, a blur of acute illness; too sick to give thanks much less experience gratitude. We had a party the Sunday before Thanksgiving and Greg, Cole and Dot came. I do not remember the party. I was too sick.

Woody and I were supposed to go to Houston for Thanksgiving with Illy and her husband Michael and their children Margot, Mari and my godson Miguel. We did not go. I was too sick. We did not do much of anything other than me being sick. I was so sick that I did not do radiation. The radiation doctors want me to resume radiation and I am concerned because I am still sick. I do not want cancer again. I do not want to die of some flu either. Everybody tells me what they recommend and I am not sure what I should do. I just know I do not want to go through any of this ever again. I am sure that Greg feels the same way about being returned to prison. We are both about as powerless over others as we could be. So we will see.

# 44

# I TOLD YOU SO

Whatever I do I do not want anyone to say to me "I told you so." I worry about not taking Tamoxifen. I worry about taking Tamoxifen. There is a lot to worry about either way. If I do not take Tamoxifen my body will continue to produce estrogen, which by the way bodies are supposed to produce. But my tumor was estrogen positive so the theory is if there is no estrogen then there is no fuel source for any tumor to grow. My cancer was also progesterone positive and her2 positive. I take Herceptin for the tumor's her2 newness. I am okay with the Herceptin. I visualize Herceptin as being duct tape and it covers the oncogene. Herceptin just puts duct tape over the oncogene's mouth so that it cannot communicate with the other oncogene's and can no longer say "Let's party and make a tumor". I will take Herceptin for another six months. The theory with that is that after a year of Herceptin when you stop taking the drug, or in my mind when you take the duct tape off the oncogene's mouth it will have forgotten what it wanted to say. It allows the cells a do over. I think that Herceptin will work.

But as to the Tamoxifen I do not want all of my estrogen to be cut off. Tamoxifen has its own side effects. None of which I want. I do not want to be depressed. I do not want bone and muscle ache. I do not want hot flashes. I do not want to worry about getting ovarian cancer because of the Tamoxifen. I also do not want to not take it and then get cancer again and then hear someone say I told you so. And therein lies my perpetual dilemma. I worry about what other people think.

I saw Brad, my oncologist a few days after meeting with Dr. Chaucer the radiologist and Lora, the breast surgeon, about my inability to complete radiation. My fever never really went away while I was on radiation. In fact it got worse and worse to the 104 point and the night I thought that I would die. It was that night that I decided that I could not continue the radiation. I know that the protocol for radiation after a lumpectomy is every workday for 6 weeks. I only did three weeks. The doctors wanted me to continue. But I knew that I was too weak and sick and the radiation zapped my body of any chance of getting the strength to get rid of the fever and the cough.

Brad wanted to talk about Tamoxifen and the other aromatose inhibitors- the estrogen blockers. According to the tables taking an estrogen blocker increases my odds against a recurrence by about ten per cent. Those are significant and Brad urged me to consider doing hormone therapy, which means taking drugs blocking my body's production of estrogen. I was still sick when I saw Brad. He saw that I was sick. I was so stirred up there was really not much he or anyone could say to me. I did not know what I should do. I knew what I wanted but I was afraid that whatever I chose would be the wrong decision and I did not want to hear from anyone and especially myself "I told you so."

I did not know what to do. So Woody and I went back to Mexico to Sanoviv. This time Woody was the primary patient and we went for her to be examined and for her to understand what is going on in her body, especially with respect to her left ovary. I went to clear my head because I could not make any decision much less a good one with the background noise going on in my head of "I told you so."

"I told you so" is right up there with the phrase "you should have". I use that phrase a lot, especially talking to clients. "You should not have said anything" is probably the one that I say the most. I am not sure it helps. I say it so if there is a future problem the person knows to exercise their Constitutional right to remain silent. But usually I end up saying, "yet again you should not have said anything". For whatever reason I was absolutely distraught with fear that I would not take Tamoxifen and then the cancer would come back and that someone, anyone, everyone would say to me "you should have taken Tamoxifen". Hearing, fearing those words was more bothersome to me than the possible return of cancer.

So that is why I went back to Mexico, to Sanoviv. I had to deal with the words in my head. I also got to see my doctor and spend time with Woody. Sanoviv is a very relaxing hospital. I began each day with exercise and meditation, some things that I do not allow myself the time when I am home but that too is changing. After seven days of meditating and relaxing at Sanoviv, in just seven days the "I told you so voice" was gone. I have been back home ten days and the voice has still not returned.

Woody and I had a great time in Sanoviv. Woody liked her doctor and her doctor spent a lot of time with her. Woody's doctor reviewed all of the films taken at Kaiser. The doctors at Sanoviv described the growth as a cyst that had arisen from an infection in Woody's fallopian tubes. A cyst sounds far less threatening than a tumor. Woody asked her doctor if the cyst could shrink without surgery. The doctor, Dr. Miriam, said it was possible but doubtful. Woody was given suggestions as to what she could do to shrink the cyst without surgery. Woody has been on a special diet. She does not eat anything that runs, flies, or swims. This means she does not eat any animal protein. Woody does not eat processed foods. Woody does not eat any sugar. Woody has stuck to her diet for over a month now. I hope it works. Woody seems at peace with her decision. That makes it easier for both of us no matter what. I think the same is true for me.

Woody has a big show set for January 26 at the Brava Theater. We started planning the event before I knew I had cancer. We started planning the event before Woody knew she had an ovarian cyst, if she even had an ovarian cyst then. I worry that she got the cyst as she watched me go through chemo. That is possible. It had to be so stressful to watch me being killed as a treatment for cancer that without the killer treatment I could die. I wish that Woody had not gotten a cyst or a tumor or whatever it is. But I am watching Woody take care of herself and I believe that her cyst is shrinking and that the show will go on and that after it is over there will be no cyst for Dr. Littell to remove. Wouldn't that be nice.

I am sure that Woody is good with her decisions about her body. I think Woody got comfortable with her decision after she went to Sanoviv. Sanoviv is brilliant and also gives time and space for people to think and reflect and make decisions based on what they are comfortable with. I think that is what Woody has done.

# 45

# TRUTH IS PEACEFUL

I am good with my decisions, meaning I am at peace with me and my decisions. It is my body and my life and these are my decisions. Each person must make their own decisions and be good with their own decisions. It is my life, my body, and I know it better than anyone. But that was not always true. When this extraordinary odyssey began I hardly paid any attention to my body. I am not sure I even liked my body. I did not feed my body regularly. I certainly did not feed it food and drink that nourishes my body. I really did not know. I am not sure that I cared. But I do care now. And I do know better. But how arrogant of me that I had lived for some 50 years without a lot of respect or connection with my body. Also that is not really very smart.

I did not have much appreciation for anything about me. I had some respect for things that I had done, but not a lot of respect for me, which is a huge difference. Now I do have respect for me, sometimes. But that takes time as well. I have to take the time to remember that even I am someone. How odd that I have to remember that I am me and that me is someone. But I do and that takes time and it was time that before I got cancer that I did not take. It is time that I think if I am to avoid a repeat journey down the cancer road that I have to take. I have to remember that I am me. I have to remember that I am me and that my "me-ness" is different than what I do. What I do reflects upon me but it is not me. And even if I do everything, whether it be climb Everest, or win a trial, or run a marathon, or get elected to Congress doing things alone will not make me okay with me. I know some people have another pathology such that whatever they do or not do they think they are great. I am the opposite of that or rather was the opposite of that. Now I just want to be right sized, sometimes great and other times not so great, but that I am aware of what is true for me.

It is easy for me to get distracted. I get distracted by work, by other people, by things, by worries, even by myself. I have to remind myself on a daily basis that I have to pay attention to myself and that I have to stay aware of what and how I think and feel. I have to do all that to keep the "I told you so" voices at bay, so that I do not get caught up in what other people think, or what I think other people think. I have to stay focused on what I think and what I feel so that I can be comfortable with myself. Because wherever I go, whatever I do, I am the one constant, which can be both a blessing and a burden. But it is usually a combination of the two and it is always still me.

My plan is to continue with the Herceptin and get those hopefully forgetful oncogenes to shut up for a year. I will not take Tamoxifen or any of the aromatose inhibitors-the estrogen blockers. I will deal with my estrogen by diminishing the amount I produce as well as improving the rate at which I metabolize what I produce. I will take calcium d glutinate and indole3 carbinol to decrease production of estrogen and improve elimination of estrogen. I have stopped eating sugar. I eat at least one serving a day of cruciferous vegetables, which somehow helps. I start each day by drinking organic lemon squeezed in boiling water with a touch of cayenne pepper. The hot lemon helps my body Ph to be alkaline and not acidic. Cancer likes acidic. So I like hot lemon.

I think I overproduce estrogen when I have temper tantrums and anger outbursts. Estrogen comes from adrenal glands as well as the ovaries. When I freak out my adrenal glands pump out adrenalin as well as estrogen. I must stop that. I do not need either the adrenalin or the estrogen and that is something that I do that I do not need to do. That will be a challenge. It is a challenge. That rush is like a drug to me. I did not even realize how accustomed I had become to the rush until I started to try and stop the outbursts. Apparently I like the rush. I must have because I did it so often.

My finger nails are terrible. That is a side effect of the chemo. My nails are weak. So when I am starting to freak out I cannot bite at or tear at my nails because they are so weak they tear into the cuticle. I do not like that my nails are so weak. I do not like that I do not have that distraction available to me and that instead I just must be me. It is getting easier. The pain of tearing my nails has made it easier. I remember that pain.

I do not know if I experienced some pain early in my life that caused me to get so disconnected from myself. Or maybe I never was connected. But I see the consequences of being disconnected now. I am not saying that I would not have gotten cancer had I been more aware of myself, of my environment, of my behavior. I do not know. But I am saying I believe that my chances of having a recurrence are greatly diminished by my newfound self awareness, my newfound knowledge of my environment and nutrition, and my commitment to acting in accord with my new awareness.

I hold the power to my life. I hold the power to my health. I hold the power to my happiness and well-being. That is the lesson that cancer has taught me. The only difficulty that I have ever really had has been my problem with being me. It has manifested itself in many different forms, some subtle some not so subtle. But the problem is inherently the same and that problem is me. Which also means that I am the solution.

The solution is as simple as appreciating that in a torrential wintry downpour, as I walked from the court to my car, as the rain was pounding and the wind blowing I felt my hair blow for the first time since it all fell out. How great to feel my hair be long enough to be blown by the wind. How great to feel my scalp move because my hair was being blown. Wind blown hair made me happy for the rest of the day and I made a point to tell anyone who wanted to hear that my hair had just blown in the wind. I have tried shaking my head to illustrate the phenomena with no luck. A head shake does not produce sufficient force to move my hair, but soon enough that will happen as well. Hopefully I will remember to celebrate the experience.

I do not know what the future holds. No one does. Maybe I will never again have to deal with cancer and treatments and maybe I will. I am frightened and I am frightened that I am frightened. I hope no one ever gets the chance to say "I told you so" to me. And even if they do I hope that I do not care because I am secure about what I have decided and why I have decided whatever it is I have decided. Then I worry about that and then I stop myself. There is no point in worrying about what other people think or what I think other people think.

I know to go back to that place in my heart where I remember that I am at peace with myself. I know that my destiny whatever it is, is mine and for that reason it is perfect for me. Perfect, for no other reason than it is mine. I am me and my destiny is mine. That is true for each of us. What works for me may not work for someone else and vice versa. I ought to concern myself with what works for me and not what others think will work for me. When all is said and done I answer to myself and really not to anyone else. That is the ultimate lesson for each of us. The problem with that is I am the one I answer to. And that is a problem because much of the time I am not aware of what I am doing. It is not very hard to answer to someone who does not know what is going on. And that is what I did for years. If I am going to have to be the one who holds me accountable then I must be vigilant in watching what I do. But when I am vigilant in the watching I do not do much that is wrong. And isn't that funny and perfect.

I told Brad, my oncologist, that I read the obituaries. I have read them a lot for a few years, well before my cancer diagnosis. I always get angry meaning disappointed when the obit does not disclose the cause of death. I think why hide it, the person is dead. So the obit is not about the dead as much as it is about some living person who decided that the dead person would care whether or not the cause of death is disclosed. Perhaps the decedent himself said he did not want the cause of death disclosed. Even that does not seem right. We all die. We should know how each other dies.

I have said for years that I want to die sober. I want to live sober but I want to live sober in part so that I can die sober. I am not being morbid. I am being practical. I think about my obituary. I told Brad that I did not want an obituary anytime soon. I said that I did not want my obituary to read that I died of cancer because I do not want to die of cancer. If I do die of cancer then that is what my obituary will say. My obituary will tell the truth whatever and whenever it is. I told Brad that I did not want the obituary to read that "I fought valiantly against cancer' or that I "bravely fought" or "finally succumbed". I do not want to fight with myself and I do not want to fight my cancer. That is what cancer is, a cellular fight with some short-circuited cells killing the good ones. But they are still all my cells. Cancer is me fighting me.

Brad said "you want your obituary to say I did it my way". Then he laughed as he meant no offense. And I said "that is not what I want. What I want is to not fight with myself." That is what I want; I want to be good with myself. I do not want to die fighting myself. I want to be at peace with anything and everything that happens.

Living life is truly an art. It is a practice and just when I think I have learned a lesson there is some new experience to teach me yet again another lesson that all seem to boil down to the same thing. That same thing is a line from a rap song Woody and I wrote a few years ago to commemorate the Hopland Womens' Music Festival.

Imagine the beat with a strong baseline and then I say with the rhythm of a wanna be rapper:

*So tell the truth*
*Be who you are*

There are other lines. It is a good rap. The other words are for the rap, not the point. The point is to tell the truth and be at peace with who I am, which means I am responsible for knowing who I am.

The point is to tell the truth and be who I am. Sometimes the truth is hard to know and sometimes it is hard for me to be who I am. I have guilt, shame and all that. But it truly is not my shame it is the shame that I give myself from what I think others think. That is what

I have learned, that the practice of life is to stay in touch with who I am, who we are.

Today I know that I am a Cancer Survivor. I hope that remains true, a day at a time, for a very long time. I hope that remains true for every day for the rest of my life. That is what I hope. And for today that is the truth and I am thrilled. That truth feels very peaceful.

# 46

# THAT IS NO WAY TO END THE BOOK

I am having trouble ending the book. I want to end the book heroically and triumphantly and mercifully not grandiosely. I am not sure that heroic and triumphant can ever be anything but grandiose. Heroic and grandiose also do not seem so true. And after a powerful line like "truth is peaceful" it is ridiculous to end the book triumphantly and heroically. Although that is what I want, that is not true.

Truth is peaceful, but life is not. Life is turbulent and volatile. Peace is perpetual. But life is until it is not. I do not want to keep writing this book until I die. And I do not want to die now just to end the book. But I do want to end the book and I want to end it true. So I will end like I started it with a short story.

Just before I found the lump in my right breast that led to the finding of the cancer in my left breast Woody and I signed papers to rent the Brava Theater for Women and the Arts. The Brava is a great old theater in San Francisco. It was originally called the York Theater as it is located at the corner of 24th and York. The Brava seats about 350 people and it is a great refurbished venue. The sound is good throughout the house. Every seat in the house is a good one for both sight and sound. We rented the theater so that Woody could have a concert to celebrate the 30th Anniversary of the release of her first album, Oregon Mountains.

We had started the process of looking for a venue and setting a date early in 2007, hoping to have the concert in the fall of 2007. Obstacle after obstacle arose regarding the setting of the date as well as selecting the venue. We chose the Brava because it is owned and operated by a nonprofit organization called Brava Theater for Women and the Arts and we are feminists, whatever that means in the 21st century. I am not sure but I do not want to digress into another diatribe. Not here. Not now. The point is in addition to being a great venue the choice was politically correct and I say that in a true way not a disparaging way. I want to support women and the Arts and I want to support women owned and operated businesses.

Once we settled upon the Brava then we tried to select a date. Each fall date we selected back in early April 2007 for one reason or another did not work. I got angry. I said to Woody things like "I cannot understand why we cannot get a date in the fall". I reasoned. I bargained and yet for one reason or another we could not get a fall date. We chose the date of January 26, 2008, about three months later than I had wanted. When Woody agreed upon the January 26 date she selected it because it worked. I knew it worked because it was the weekend between the National Football League Championship game and the Super Bowl. That was important to me. I doubt it was important to anyone else but it worked for me.

All that happened just a few days before Woody's birthday and the discovery of the lump in my right breast that led to the call to the doctor that led to the mammogram that showed the cancer in my left breast. Had I gotten the date I originally wanted, sometime in September 2007 I would have still been sick from chemo and the operation. I doubt we would have been able to do the concert. The date not being available had upset me. Then in the end the date not being available was the best thing that ever could have happened. Therein lies another one of life's lessons that I have experienced repeatedly and until this experience refused to learn. That everything happens for the best. Even when I do not see it that way in the long run everything happens for the best.

We did not work so much on concert production while I was doing Chemo. I wrote this book and was sick. Woody watched me be sick and she practiced. Woody practiced the piano. Woody practiced the guitar. Woody practiced singing. Woody practiced the banjo. It was fun listening and watching Woody play. The music soothed me. The music soothed Woody. I used to play the guitar a bit. But I was too sick to play. So I listened and listened. Woody wrote a new banjo song called Sailor Girl. Woody decided that song would open the show. Woody finished the song somewhere toward the end of August just before my surgery. That is when the show became real. I started to worry about how we would fill the 350 Brava seats. Then instead of worrying we went to work.

Just as we were underway in concert preparation Woody was given the news about her ovarian tumor. Woody chose to delay the surgery as Dr. Littel could not guarantee that he could do the surgery laporoscopically. He had reassured us that the growth, whatever it was, was not cancerous. The doctors at Sanoviv also said they thought whatever it was, it was not cancerous. So it was safe to wait. Woody did her special no animal protein diet and put castor oil packs over her liver three days in a row every other week. And we worked on the concert.

Suffice to say we did everything we could throughout the fall to prepare for the show. We sent out emails and press releases. Our friends sent out emails and press releases. Woody mailed CDs to radio stations. We plastered posters around town. Suze Orman posted a notice on her web site. Suze gets tons of hits on her web site. We hired a recording engineer. We hired someone to film the show. We invited great musicians to play. We got great hotel rooms for the out of town players. We made travel arrangements. We hired a caterer for the pre-show meal.

A rehab facility that I work with called Jericho Project came over to the theater a few days before the show and cleaned and painted the green room and the dressing rooms. We got some furniture for the balcony in the green room. The green room is the room that performers wait in before they go on stage. I have no idea why it is called a green room. I have been in many green rooms for all of the local television stations and cable stations and one national network and not one has been green. Regardless of the "why" Jericho Project painted the green room pale yellow and made it look really nice.

Debra Walker designed t-shirts and did the graphics for the program. We ordered pins from Nepal of the Buddhist knot, which signifies love and made schwag bags for all of the players and helpers. The schwag bag contained the pin, hair care products from Italy, Woody's newest CD, a program, a t-shirt, and some cash. I designed the schwag bags.

On January 26, 2008 Woody had her 30$^{th}$ anniversary Oregon Mountains Concert. The concert was awesome. It was the best concert I have ever been to. I enjoyed myself from start to finish. The seats were filled. 350 people and then some came to the show.

I invited all of my many doctors and all of my friends who helped me go through my difficult summer. Most all of them came. And the invited musicians came. Cris Williamson, Laura Love, Jen Todd, Laurie Lewis, Nancy Vogel, Christine Bagley, Patty Vincent, Jeri Jones, Marca Cassity, Kitty Rose, Katrina Spang-Hanssen, Stephanie Lee, Jan Martinelli, Amy Myers, and Robin Roth came and played. They shined and they helped Woody shine.

The show started with Suze introducing Woody. Suze looked great, really great. Suze radiates light and is very funny at times and this was one of those times. Suze introduced Woody who was joined by Laurie Lewis. Woody on her banjo and Laurie on her fiddle played Sailor Girl, the song that I was sick by. It never sounded better, which was partly a combination of the duo playing and the fact that I am no longer sick from chemo or cancer or anything. I did not worry at all during the show because for that evening I truly believed that whatever happened would be perfect for no other reason than it was happening.

Before a show there is always a lot of energy. Everyone is nervous in some form or another. This night was like every other and like no other. Everyone was nervous. Everyone wanted to perform well and yet everyone was really happy. Being around performers and performing on television is relatively new to me. I have always been around locker rooms and had performance anxiety before each and every sporting event I ever played in, from swimming meets as a child to power lifting competitions as an adult. This was kind of like that, but fun.

That night I drove to the theater by myself. I had driven Woody to the theater earlier in the day and arranged for the transport of the players from the hotel to the theater. They had to get there early to do sound check and get ready and do those things that performers do before a performance.

I went back home and took a bath. I was alone for the first time in such a long time. The house was quiet. My heart was pounding with excitement and nerves for Woody. But I sat in the bath and asked myself how did I want this experience to be. I decided I did not want to have a nervous dramatic night. I decided I wanted a fun and accepting night that whatever happened would be perfect and that I would enjoy it and be grateful for getting to be a part of Woody's life and the lives of so many wonderful people.

I drove to the theater in the Cadillac Escalade. That is one big car/ truck and looked for a place to park. I was late, an hour before show time and there were no parking spaces. I did not freak out. I stayed calm and prayed by repeating a phrase I call my mantra. My mantra is in Sanskrit and it means I honor the God that dwells within me. I said it over and over and then I saw a man pulling out of a parking place and asked him if I could have his spot and then realized another person was waiting for the spot. I told the waiter to go ahead and take the spot, that he had been there first, no worries. I was so calm I really meant it, no worries. But the waiting man then insisted I take the parking place. He smiled at me and insisted again. I thanked him and took the spot and thanked him again. He smiled. I smiled. That is the power of me being me and accepting whatever is happening. I went into the theater with that feeling and sat down and had the time of my life.

After the first song Suze re-entered the stage and introduced Democrat State Senator Carole Migden who presented Woody with a Senate resolution recognizing Woody's thirty years of writing, performing, and producing music for the women's community in particular and for all in general. On stage Suze bantered with Woody, who bantered with Suze, who bantered with Carole, and the three of them had an unabashedly good time in a love fest with all of us watching.

Then the music really began and the two act 17 song show was over in a nanosecond. I was mesmerized and completely present for the night. I did not worry. I did not stress. I did not even think about Vanessa Redgrave or anyone else for that matter. Of my many friends who were there for the night's festivities I did not wish for, nor worry about anyone who was there or not there. I did not used to do that. I used to worry about almost everything. It used to be nothing was good enough, especially me. Now when I am clear headed I know that everything is perfect. Just like that night, it was a perfect night. I had a perfect night. I think that everyone had a perfect night. It was a night of joyful music and so fun. I am so glad that we had that night. It was a perfect night because I had absolutely no difficulty being me, nor did I have any difficulty with anyone being who they are, nor did anyone seem ill at ease with being themselves. No one suffered from DWBM (difficulty with being me). Everyone was perfect.

The show was so perfect that for weeks we received emails and phone calls and letters telling us how great the show had been. Somewhere in all of the hoopla Woody had another ultrasound that showed that her tumor had shrunk in half meaning that it was benign. So she will wait and see and continue with her diet regimen and castor oil packs. That is what I will do as well.

The days come and go. My hair grows a little each day. Not much seems to bother me. Right now everything is looking good. Right now everything is perfect. Which is, of course, the perfect ending.